T0368866

BORIS JOHNSON

THE
NEVERENDING
TORY

www.penguin.co.uk

BORIS JOHNSON

THE
NEVERENDING
TORY

THE ADVENTURE WHERE
YOU TAKE BACK CONTROL

IAIN HOLLINGSHEAD

bantam

TRANSWORLD PUBLISHERS
Penguin Random House, One Embassy Gardens,
8 Viaduct Gardens, London SW11 7BW
www.penguin.co.uk

Transworld is part of the Penguin Random House group of companies
whose addresses can be found at global.penguinrandomhouse.com

First published in Great Britain in 2022 by Bantam
an imprint of Transworld Publishers

Copyright © Iain Hollingshead 2022

Iain Hollingshead has asserted his right under the Copyright,
Designs and Patents Act 1988 to be identified as the author of this work.

Every effort has been made to obtain the necessary permissions with
reference to copyright material, both illustrative and quoted. We apologize
for any omissions in this respect and will be pleased to make the
appropriate acknowledgements in any future edition.

A CIP catalogue record for this book
is available from the British Library.

ISBN 9781787636927

Typeset in 12/16pt Plantin MT Pro by Jouve (UK), Milton Keynes.
Text design by Couper Street Type Co.
Printed and bound in Great Britain by Clays Ltd, Elcograf S.p.A.

The authorized representative in the EEA is Penguin Random House Ireland,
Morrison Chambers, 32 Nassau Street, Dublin D02 YH68.

Penguin Random House is committed to a sustainable future
for our business, our readers and our planet. This book is made
from Forest Stewardship Council® certified paper.

To Ali, my beloved current wife,
and to all my legally recognized children

Children of all ages love
Boris Johnson: The Neverending Tory

*'I read the endings where he doesn't become
Prime Minister again and again.'*
T. May, age 66, Maidenhead

*'I have never been Prime Minister, but this book gave
me the chance to see what it might be like.'*
J. Corbyn, age 73, The Allotment, North London

'You're joking – not another one.'
Brenda from Bristol

'I cried so hard I almost laughed.'
D. Cameron, age 56, The Shepherd's Hut, Oxfordshire

*'It's a real page-turner, which is the best
way of staying warm this winter.'*
J. Rees-Mogg, age 53, Somerset

*'This book is excellent value for money –
if your salary is paid in US dollars.'*
K. Kwarteng, age 47, London

'I have nothing memorable to say about this book.'
L. Truss, age 47, London

'No one builds statues to writers of multiple-choice adventure books.'
World King B. Johnson, age 58, South London

'It was nice to get to know my father better.'
Anon

BORIS JOHNSON

THE
NEVERENDING
TORY

WARNING!

This book is different from other books.

There are dangers, choices and consequences.

But you are different from other people. And it will mainly be other people dealing with the consequences of your choices.

You must use your many talents: buffoonery, polygamy, bogus self-deprecation, limitless ambition, an artfully distressed wardrobe and a Wikipedia page of classical references you half remember from school. The wrong choice could end in tragedy – even death. Or worse, political death. But don't worry. At any time you can go back and make another decision, changing the direction and the result of your story.

Just like writing two newspaper columns.

In twenty minutes.

For £250,000 p.a.

To determine the future of a country.

And then deciding which column you prefer.

And then cocking it all up regardless.

Anyway.

Not your problem.

Aut Caesar aut nihil.

Yes, you might need a Latin dictionary handy.

It means: 'Either Emperor or nothing.'

Now get your own dictionary.

But what if Emperor is insufficient? What if you want to fulfil your childhood ambition to become World King, a position so important that you will have to invent it first?

Yes, this is your lifelong quest.

And it won't be easy.

You will encounter demons and dragons, monsters and maidens – and Liz Truss.

You will be blighted by the Blob, entranced by Trump, bewitched by a sorceress called Carrie, captivated by your backbench Orcs – and royally shafted by a little hobgoblin called Michael Gove.

Not everyone wants you to be World King.

Come to think of it, no one does.

But you will have a lot of fun trying.

Like Bastian in *The Neverending Story*, the tale of an unhappy little boy who makes up stories, can't control his desires and loses his way in a mythical world of many-headed beasts, betrayed friendships and a Childlike Empress called Margaret Thatcher.

Or Lancelot missing out on the Holy Grail because he was knocking off someone else's wife.

Yes, this, too, is the story of one person, known to millions by just his first name. Like Hannibal. Or Madonna. Or Jesus.

It is the second Greatest Story Ever Told.

A story of great sacrifice: of principles; of relationships. A story of Fleet Street legend: the *Daily Telegraph*'s Brussels Correspondent and Sacked *Times* Journalist Trainee Who Would be King.

A story of great love(s): a smattering of *ludus*; more *eros* than you can shake a pole-dancer at; and, at its centre, a beautiful blond blob of *philautia*.

Yes, you, of course, are the hero of this story.

But you knew that already, didn't you?

1

You are born Alexander Boris de Pfeffel Johnson, on 19 June 1964, weighing 4.1kg (sorry, 9lb 1oz), in New York City. Technically speaking, this means that you can be US President . . . is your first sentient thought on emerging, blinking, from the womb.

You will return to this thought later.

Right now you are interrupted by a knock on the door.

You have visitors.

Three Wise Men, perhaps, bearing gifts of Good Old British Common Sense, Mirth and Enough Gold to Get a Place at a Decent British Prep School?

No, it is your father.

Your mother holds you out to him, asking if he wants to sever the umbilical cord that ties you to the overly centralized, bureaucratic, undemocratic, federalist, welfarist, socialist nightmare of an organ that is her placenta.

Your father eagerly takes the scissors, unconscious of the irony that your Brexit policy will one day force him to become a French citizen.

'He looks just like Churchill,' he says.

Your eyes light up.

'We should put him down at birth,' he continues.

'He's not that bad,' your mother protests.

'For Eton, I meant,' your father adds hastily. 'They will raise him as if their own child until he is ready to claim his birthright.'

Your birthright?

You feel the strength of your manifest destiny coursing through your veins. Your blood is already royal and racy: your maternal grandmother has illegitimate links to George II; your paternal great-grandfather, Ali Kemal, was a four-times-married Turkish politician-journalist lynched by a mob he had once courted.

There is an irony here.

Later you will claim that Kemal's son, your grand-father, was a British asylum seeker.

This is not true.[1]

A midwife enters the room. 'It's outside visiting hours,' she says, pointing at a sign on the wall.

'But it's his birthday,' says your father, winking at you.

'Rules are rules,' she says.

'I am sure that whatever happened, the guidance was followed and the rules were followed at all times,' you say.[2]

'His first words!' says your father. 'I'm so proud!'

But no one is listening.

Your father is ushered out and you are alone with

your mother. She leans over to tickle you under your chins.

Are you hungry, she wonders?

If you want to Get Breakfast Done, turn to episode 2

If you decide to fall asleep on the job, turn to episode 3

2

You signify the end of your breakfast with a loud, satisfying sign of appreciation.

This is not the last time you will shit the bed.

The midwife returns to change your nappy. You giggle and pee in her eye.

This is not the last time your Excalibur sword will get you into trouble.

Turn to episode 3

3

You lead a life of 'blameless, panda-like passivity'[3] until your sister, Rachel, is born fourteen months later, galvanizing you into a state of frenzied sibling rivalry that will provide excellent training for a life in politics.

Some might compare your sister to Morgan le Fay, the goddess protector of her eldest brother who is destined to become World King (a childhood secret you certainly don't regret her sharing in almost every newspaper interview since).

Others will refer to her as a bestselling novelist and journalist – and winner of the Bad Sex in Fiction Award, 2008.

Or the *Celebrity Big Brother* contestant in 2018 who was beaten by Ann Widdecombe – and almost everyone else.

Or the lead candidate for Change UK for the South West England constituency in the 2019 European Parliament election who was beaten by Ann Widdecombe – and almost everyone else.

Just don't introduce her as your sister.

Even if that's the main thing she writes about

(including an unusual sisterly observation, during communal childhood showers, that you have an abnormally large willy).

Over the years your father, a politician turned journalist, will sire a total of six children, including Jo, a journalist turned politician turned journalist.

Where *does* your family get its ideas from?

We will come back to Rachel later.

What should everyone else call *you*?

You Can Call Me Al: turn to episode 52

If you're not yet sure about your name, turn to episode 64

4

You make yourself helpful during the 2015 general election campaign by writing an article about Old Etonian Prime Ministers.

'The next PM will be Miliband if you don't fucking shut up,' texts Sir Dave, gratefully.[4]

But he's wrong about this – just as he's wrong about almost everything else.

The following year he decides to honour his manifesto commitment to heal an unhealable rift in the Conservative Party by opening up an unhealable rift in the country.

Leave or Remain? You're in a genuine quandary, 'veering all over the place like a broken shopping trolley'.[5]

What would the Childlike Empress do? She signed the Single European Act in 1986. But she also said 'No, No, No' to The Nothing.

So would she fight the enemy from without, like the Argentinians? Or the enemy from within, like the miners?

If only you could ask her.

You're going to have to do this alone.

But what's the right thing for the newly elected goblin for Uxbridge and South Ruislip and part-time Mayor of London to do?

More importantly, what's the most expedient thing for the newly elected goblin for Uxbridge and South Ruislip and part-time Mayor of London to do?

If you support Leave and they win, you'll probably be Prime Minister.

If you support Remain and they win, Sir Dave will make you Foreign Secretary.

But who *is* going to win?

Time to write two articles and see which one you find more convincing.

If you rally round the Remain campaign, turn to episode 34

If you decide to spearhead the Leave campaign, turn to episode 79

5

Yes, it's coming back to you now. A murky memory of a murky conversation the wrong side of midnight.

'Mr Johnson, we know everything about you.'

'So does everyone,' you slur. 'And still they love me.'

That is your greatest wish granted so far by the Childlike Empress's amulet. To be loved.

'No, Mr Johnson, we know *everything*.'

'Oh.'

That's a very different kettle of *ukha*.

Your head is still pounding as the plane begins its descent over the English Channel. The only other thing you can remember from last night is the word *Kompromat* being repeated again and again.

The plane touches down on the runway. You turn on your phone and double-check the definition of the Russian word.

Compromising material, gathered on individuals for the purpose of blackmail.

You're just reading about all the interesting people who have supposedly been targeted by the FSB, from Russian prosecutor generals to American presidents-elect, when a message appears on your phone.

'We'll be in touch,' it says.

You delete it and bury your throbbing head in your shaking hands.

Turn to episode 88

6

You meet a British expat editor of the *San Francisco Bee* at a party in Georgetown, DC. Captivated by your dismissal of the 'snivelling, fact-grubbing historians'[6] who unearthed your fabricated quote about Edward II, she offers you a job as Washington correspondent of the West Coast broadsheet.

The problem with American journalism, she says, is that it takes itself too seriously. No one wants to hear about the Soviet withdrawal from Afghanistan or the new Prime Minister of Pakistan or the Polish trade union movement.

Stuff Solidarity, she says. Bugger Bhutto.

People want pizzazz, not Pulitzers. Entertainment. Stories.

You agree. You have a lot of stories.

Oh, so many stories.

Congress, you report, cheekily, wants to ban round grapes in the Golden State.

The Food and Drug Administration, you report, has withdrawn its approval for the sale of condoms in Austin because penises in the Lone Star State are too small ('Californian Cocks Trump Tiny Texan Todgers').

The unelected, federalist, faceless Supreme Court, you report, wants to rule California directly.

Despite none of these stories being entirely true, you become a hero to a fringe group of San Francisco secessionists who want to leave the United States of America.

If you dismiss them as fruitcakes, loonies and closet racists, turn to episode 14

If you keep your cards close to your chest about your own views on Calexit, turn to episode 72

7

After two years at a prep school in Sussex, you win a scholarship to Eton, where you are excelling in classics, rugby, debating and winding up the beaks with your failure to deliver on your promise(s).

You are also good at: the Wall Game, which is played only at Eton; reciting Latin to your peers while wearing a gown, which is done only at Eton; getting elected to Pop, a prefect body which exists only at Eton; and preparing to run the world, an activity confined mainly to Eton.

One day, you tell yourself, they will replace the marble busts in Upper School of Canning, Pitt, Gladstone, Macmillan, Orwell, Keynes and the rest of those drop-outs with one giant statue of World King Boris.

In the meantime, your classical education is allowing you to gather the loyal companions you will need for your quest. Pericles, Margaret Thatcher, Bertie Wooster, Molesworth – these are the diverse heroes you will call upon to bring order to a troubled land.

(You have lots of real friends at school too. But

we dare not mention them for libel reasons. And in case you offer to give their heavies our address.)

What do you admire so much about the classical world? Is it Rome's heroes, feted by the crowds? The Greek myths of gods and monsters, winners and losers, death and glory? The mastery of language? The ability it confers to hoodwink the masses?

Maybe you will tell us about it one day.

Meanwhile, your housemaster notes your big helping of personal charm, the risk of appointing you Captain of School given your lack of interest in administrative tasks, your occasional gross failure of responsibility, your exceptional belief that you should be 'free of the network of obligation which binds everyone else' and your lazy assumption that 'success and honours will drop into your lap'.[7]

If you decide to act upon his useful advice, turn to episode 76

If you ignore him, turn to episode 36

8

You're beginning to get the hang of this.

Wine Friday to 'stay alert'.

Karaoke to 'control the virus'.

Office fights to 'save lives'.

On 13 November 2020 Carrie finally persuades you that you'll have more chance of calling yourself the Childlike Emperor if you banish Dominic Cummings to the Land of the Blogs. He leaves quietly through one of the most famous doors in the world holding a large cardboard metaphor.

What does Leave mean?

Leave means Leaving Party, of course.

Even if you can't really cope without your Luckdragon.

Even if you did reluctantly announce a second lockdown eight days earlier.

Best call it a leaving 'meeting' then.

Start the meeting at 6 p.m., after the end of the working day, in the Downing Street hobbit-hole, where you live.

Invite people delighted to see the back of Cummings.

Join the meeting yourself at 8 p.m.
Continue 'discussions' late into the evening.
Make alcohol freely available at the meeting.
Take no minutes at the meeting.
Crank up the Abba at the meeting.
No. Nothing for Sue Gray to see here.

Turn to episode 30

9

In 1872 William Gladstone had a letter published in *The Spectator*. Between 1876 and 1884 Herbert Asquith wrote sixty articles for the magazine. In 1999 you go one stage further than these two previous Prime Ministers by becoming editor.

The Spectator thrives on your watch. The publisher has an affair with the Home Secretary. Your executive editor has an affair with the receptionist. And your deputy editor has an affair with you (your dismissal of this 'inverted pyramid of piffle' turns out to be an 'inverted pyramid of piffle' – also known as 'absolute bullshit').[8]

You even publish some articles.

Some of them don't lead to apologies to major northern cities.

You're on the up.

You're the darling of the libertarian Right.

The Childlike Empress's amulet is working.

Your wishes are slowly becoming true.

Suddenly, there is a knock at the door.

Is it Conrad Black, the owner of *The Spectator*, come to check whether this 'very cunning operator, a fox disguised as a teddy bear',[9] is going to renege on his promise not to pursue any political ambitions while editing the magazine?

Or one of the wronged damsels of the Knights of the Round Conference Table, delivering ten sacks of manure to your Doughty Street office?

Or two of your writers looking for background colour for *Who's the Daddy?*, their play about *The Spectator*'s office affairs, which, in their own words, portrays the male characters as 'ludicrous and unattractive specimens, ruled by their libidos, and apt to be exploited by the good-looking, high-status females at the office'.[10]

Or David Blunkett's dog?

No. It's the producer of *Have I Got News for You*, come to offer you another lightweight guest presenter slot.

If you decide to—

Actually, no, there is no decision to make here. The show has four million viewers. Of course you'll go on it.

Turn to episode 12

10

Taking inspiration from the Japanese soldier who remained at his post for twenty years after the end of the Second World War, you decide to stay in your cosy hobbit-hole in Downing Street for as long as you can, despite the fifty-seven ministerial resignations.

After all, you single-handedly won an election in 2019, didn't you?

And you've still got Important Things to Think About in the summer of discontent of 2022.

A cost of living crisis.

Record temperatures.

Your imminent wedding at Chequers.

'Either you stay or I go,' says Princess Xayide.

That settles it.

By the weekend you've removed the whip from 121 disloyal Conservative goblins – and still found sufficient stooges among the remaining 225 to fill 109 ministerial posts.

All 109 of them have resigned by the following weekend.

This maths is getting tight.

So you go on holiday in Ukraine.

Half the Labour goblins go on strike in protest – but no one notices until Sir Keir suspends them for joining a picket line.

All eyes turn to the 1922 Committee. Will their newly elected members allow another leadership challenge?

They do – despite the *Mail* printing the home addresses of their children's teachers.

You run yourself – and lose the Tory leadership to Rishi, who travels the country in his £3,500 Henry Herbert suits offering to steal from the poor to give to Tunbridge Wells.

But still you refuse to stand down as Prime Minister.

You change the locks on your hobbit-hole and barricade yourself upstairs in Number 10, armed with a magic pea shooter that doesn't work.

You call Volodymyr to see if he's got any spares.

Then you take the phone off the hook.

In September 2022 an exasperated House of Goblins finally votes for a general election, which Labour wins in a landslide.

You become the first incumbent Prime Minister ever to lose your own seat.

But you don't mind too much because at least you and Carrie had your wedding at Chequers.

Mission largely accomplished.

Turn to episode 23

11

It's 1987 and you stand on the brink of adulthood –
or what normally passes for adulthood – with two
passports, one wife and all the attributes necessary to
become US President, British Prime Minister and/or
World King.

(Then again, you went to Eton and Oxford, so
what did you expect?)

But now it's going to get a lot more difficult.

You still lack the magical powers you'll need for
your quest.

You lack sufficient loyal companions.

And although you don't know it yet, there are
only a few ways you can meet the Childlike Empress
and access the mythical world of Fantastica.

Only a handful of routes to becoming Childlike
Emperor yourself.

Or World King.

And only two happy endings.

So choose carefully.

As you once said: 'There are no disasters, only opportunities. And, indeed, opportunities for fresh disasters.'[11]

If you want to use your US citizenship to Make America Great Again, turn to episode 37

If you decide to put the Great Back into Britain, turn to episode 33

12

Your seven appearances on *Have I Got News for You* make you a firm favourite with viewers, who warm to your bumbling, self-deprecating manner, your habit of messing up your hair just before the cameras roll and the charming way you deflect accusations that you offered to help a schoolfriend beat up a journalist.

You are nominated for a BAFTA for Best Entertainment Performance.

You lose to Jonathan Ross.

If you decide to get your revenge on Ross, turn to episode 38

If you decide to focus on politics, turn to episode 31

13

'Take that!' you yell at Rachel, peppering her with unbuilt plastic hospitals. 'And that! And that! NO ONE insults the World King.'

Your sister runs out of the room to plot Rachel's Revenge, leaving you alone with your Boris Bricks.

Boris.

You try your middle name out on your tongue.

It tastes good.

It tastes of success.

You really meant it when you told Rachel you wanted to be World King.

This is your quest.

But you're still only five.

So you're going to need some training in the Dark Arts of global kingship first.

It's almost time to go to Eton.

Turn to episode 7

14

You have just alienated half the electorate. Your American Dream is over.

Turn to episode 33

15

You roll up your sleeve and blink in the glare of the television lights as your Chief Alchemist, Professor Whitty, descends on you with a needle.

A producer holds up a board with the estimated viewing figures.

Thirty million!

This is more than watched William and Kate's wedding.

This is brilliant.

'Next slide, please,' hisses Whitty. He's not at all happy about this.

You feel a sharp prick in your arm.

'You see?' you tell everyone cowering on their sofas at home, wondering how to make sourdough out of loo roll. 'There's nothing to worry about.'

Two days later you briefly wonder whether it's a good idea for an overweight fifty-five-year-old Prime Minister injected with Covid to visit a vulnerable nonagenarian monarch at the start of a global pandemic.

Then you go anyway.

The End

16

In 2005 you reluctantly support Sir Dave for the leadership of the party. After all, he reflects many of your heroic virtues – social liberalism, membership of the Bullingdon Club and a mild dislike of The Nothing of Europe – as well as possessing a few that you lack: monogamy, truthfulness, membership of the Piers Gaveston dining club at Oxford and the ability to chillax.

No one said you had to replace the Childlike Empress straight away. If you bide your time, you can be the heir to the heir to Blair.

Recognizing your popularity with a youth demographic that will later turn on you, Sir Dave makes you Shadow Higher Education Minister, a role that allows you to tour the country and meet young satyrs and nymphs (but mainly nymphs).

You have another affair. You write another book (about Rome, inevitably). You present a TV series. In 2007 you're the third-highest-earning Member of the House of Goblins.

But still there's an insatiable itch to scratch. Another wish to wish from the silver amulet of the Golden-eyed Commander of Wishes.

You live in London. You work in London. Why not have a crack at running London, a city with a higher GDP than Spain, Mexico or Indonesia?

Enter Lynton Crosby, the master Australian election strategist, the Wizard of Oz.

'You've failed at everything so far,' the Wizard tells you.[12]

He attempts to keep you on a tight leash. Clear policies. Routemasters. Alcohol bans on the Tube. No jokes.

You even suspend *Sikanda*, your magical *Telegraph* column, while you campaign. 'I am laying down my pen,' you say, 'and taking up the sword full time.'[13]

'Boring,' say your cheerleaders in the media. 'Your pen[is] is mightier than your sword. Don't listen to Lynton. Let Boris be Boris.'

If you decide to listen to Lynton, turn to episode 74

If you let Boris be Boris, also turn to episode 74

17

The summer of 2012 is an Olympian success. Spectators particularly enjoy the way you base the New York Games more closely on its Ancient Athenian origins, reintroducing jousting, chariot racing and the Pankration, a no-holds-barred combination of boxing and wrestling in which contestants take part naked.

They're less impressed when you take part naked yourself.

Regardless, your quest is thriving. You're now being spoken of as a future President.

Modestly, you say: 'If, like the Roman leader Cincinnatus, I were to be called from my plough to serve in that office I wouldn't, of course, say no.'[14]

They say: 'What?'

Humbly, you add: 'If the ball came loose from the back of a scrum – which it won't – it would be a great, great thing to have a crack at.'[15]

They say: 'What the—?'

So you decide to show more interest in Americana to make yourself relatable. You have your teeth done. You employ a therapist, who is even more eager to talk about your childhood than your biographers are. You put on five stone – and then lose nine more. You coach Little League Baseball, knocking a ten-year-old boy unconscious while attempting to tag him out.

The delighted crowds chant: 'Hey, hey, ABJ, how many kids did you fell today?'[16]

During the 2013 New York mayoral campaign, you promise that you will serve your next term in full without any distractions.

But then you catch the eye of President (Hillary) Clinton, who defeated Barack Obama in 2008 after you ruthlessly mocked him every night on your chat shows. Charmed by your description of her 'dyed blonde hair, pouty lips and steely blue stare, like a sadistic nurse in a mental hospital',[17] she offers you the position of Secretary of State in her second administration.

If you accept Clinton's offer and break your promise, turn to episode 32

If you decline her offer and remain Mayor of New York, turn to episode 20

18

You spend a few months licking your wounds: writing your memoirs, putting some 'hay in the loft',[18] dashing off a few newspaper columns and posting unpleasant anonymous comments under Rishi Sunak's Twitter feed.

By spring 2023 you're feeling restless. Liz Truss's approval ratings are minus 60, but it's difficult to mount a challenge from outside the House of Goblins. When a Tory Orc stands down for accidentally watching snuff films in the chamber while trying to pay his credit card bill, you make tentative enquiries about contesting his seat. But your heart isn't really in it.

You need a bigger stage.

You wonder about running for US President, before remembering that you renounced your citizenship back in 2016 after being hit with an 'absolutely outrageous' tax demand by the IRS on the sale of your Islington home.[19]

And then the call comes.

Would you like to be Secretary General of NATO?

If you say yes, turn to episode 91

If you're not sure, turn to episode 50

19

'Fuck business'[20] – management consultancy is not for you.

After a brief spell at *The Times*, where you are sacked for making up a quote, you join the *Daily Telegraph*, where you are not sacked for making up whole stories.

Like Bastian in *The Neverending Story*, you have finally found your *Sikanda*, your magical weapon: it is your infuriating ability to conjure well-paid words to your whim to a deadline (or just after the deadline).

This *Sikanda* will provide a huge boost to your quest.

Thus armed with only pen and penis, in 1989 you venture bravely into the hostile foreign lands known as Brussels, where you enjoy 'chucking rocks over the garden wall and listening to this amazing crash from the greenhouse next door over in England'.[21]

Are you Pyornkrachzark, the legendary rock chewer? No, you're Brussels correspondent of the *Daily Telegraph*, one of the Sauron-like newspaper groups among the All-Seeing, All-Knowing Right-Wing Media.

One person enjoying these rocks is a ruler of near-mythical importance, known variously as Attila the Hen, the Immaculate Misconception, the Milk Snatcher, the Iron Lady and Ding, Dong, the Witch is Still Alive.

To you and the Govester, however, Margaret Thatcher will always be the Childlike Empress.

Who gives life to all creatures in the political world of Fantastica.

Who quashes Britain's enemies from Brixton to Bruges to the *Belgrano*.

Who is eventually brought low by a Cabinet revolt led by two former Chancellors of the Exchequer whose lives she had made intolerable. (There might be a lesson here.)

Who might one day need an heir to continue her work.

The Childlike Empress loves your articles from Brussels so much that they're regularly included in her briefing papers.

Finally, you have caught her attention.

One mythical night, she appears to you in your dreams.

Only you, she whispers, can be her hero.

Only you can make Fantastica reborn.

Only you can defeat 'The Nothing' of European federalism which sprawls from the Howling Forest of Ireland to the Misty Mountains of Finland.

The Nothing is making her ill.

Only you can save her.

She gives you her amulet, a silver clasp from her handbag, to show that you act on her behalf. You turn it over and read the inscription: 'Do what you wish.'

You like the sound of that.

'You can have as many wishes as you like,' whispers the Golden-eyed Commander of Wishes.

This is getting better and better.

And then she's gone, flickering briefly like a will-o'-the-wisp, before vanishing, as if she'd never been there.

Was it a dream? Did you imagine it all?

No. You feel her cold amulet in your hands. You hang it round your neck, where it nestles next to your heart. Your true quest is taking shape. It is to enter the mythical world of Fantastica. To wield your *Sikanda* in the Right-Wing Media. To avenge the lily-livered Knights of the Long Europhile Knives.

One day, en route to being World King, you might even rule this Fantastica yourself.

'Childlike Emperor'. That has a nice ring to it.

But not yet.

The electoral maths doesn't stack up.

And there are others, who will have to be destroyed, who will want this prize too.

So first, in 1999, you decide to use your *Sikanda* as editor of *The Spectator*.

Turn to episode 9

20

The joke begins to wear off in your third term as Mayor of New York.

A massive sex scandal erupts in the tabloids.

Your wife changes the locks. You change wives.

Your poll ratings start to plummet.

Donald Trump defeats Clinton in 2016. If you're going to challenge him in 2020, you're going to need to turn this around.

You need money.

You need Michael Gove, the hobgoblin who has been making waves without you in Britain's Fantastica.

Seeing your predicament, he gets in touch with his old Oxford friend with a musical ode he has written called 'Boris on Broadway'.

You perform the opening rap yourself at the premiere:

> And the world's gonna know your name.
> What's your name . . .?
> Alexander B. Johnson,
> My name is Alexander B. Johnson.[22]

The musical receives near-universal critical acclaim. Eleven Tony Awards. A Pulitzer Prize for Drama. Broadway box office records smashed. Further productions in London, Sydney and Hamburg.

And so, like an unflushable turd, you rise.

In 2020 you enter the presidential race.

Turn to episode 58

21

You push aside the mouldy food containers, the IKEA bags, the children's books, the unwashed clothes, the political leaflets and your copy (perhaps the only copy) of Liz Truss's book *Britannia Unchained* and attempt to make yourself comfortable with a bottle of Pinot on the back seat of your Toyota Previa.

Acting on a tip-off, Theresa May tells Amber Rudd to tell Cressida Dick to send a policeman to arrest you under Section 5 of the Road Traffic Act 1988.

'But I'm not in charge of the vehicle,' you say.

'You're not in charge of anything, sonny,' he says.

You're thrown into a dungeon deep below Tortoise Shell Mountain, where gigantic night-hobs torture you for the next ten years by reading you *Guardian* editorials through the loudspeaker system.

The End

22

Your unsuccessful celebrity intervention in the EU referendum of 2016 inspires you to put your celebrity money where your considerable mouth is and run for elected office.

After more than a decade in London media luvviedom, your natural home is the Labour Party. However, your repeated jokes on *Top Gear* about Jeremy Corbyn lead you to join your sister in the Lib Dems instead.

In 2017 you replace Tim Whatshisname as leader, stating that you have absolutely no problem reconciling your faith and your politics.

In 2019, with trust in politics at an all-time low, your sister asks you to join Change UK, the breakaway centrist party.

If you say yes, turn to episode 83

If you say no, turn to episode 68

23

In September 2023 you start a new chapter of your life by starring on *Strictly Come Dancing*, hoping to fill the loveable klutz slot popularized by John Sergeant, Ann Widdecombe and Ed Balls.

You're voted off in the first round.

In the winter you appear on *I'm a Celebrity*. After eating a bull's penis, a lamb's brain and three of the Rt Hon. Nadine Dorries's toenails, you're the first person to leave the jungle, lasting two fewer days than Lembit Öpik.

The media work begins to dry up in 2024.

So you go low – really low.

A Christmas special of *Take Me Out*, in which you're blacked out in the first round.

A guest appearance on *Peppa Pig*.

An unforgettable stint as a cat on *Celebrity Big Brother*, purring as you rub up against Penny Mordaunt's leg.

Boris and Carrie's Saturday Night Takeaway.

Question Time.

One day the producers suddenly stop calling.

The public has grown tired of you.

From 2025 they mete out the ultimate punishment by deciding to ignore you for the rest of your life.

Banished to the mythical City of Old Emperors, you wander the lonely streets with the rest of the lost souls who wanted to rule Fantastica but were unable to find their way back to the human world.

The End

24

Cast out of Downing Street by Michael Gove, you spend the Christmas of 2019 eating, drinking and muttering *Omnium consensu capax imperii, nisi imperasset* ('Everyone thought him capable of being the Childlike Emperor until he was shafted by a hobgoblin').

But then in January you see a blog by Dominic Cummings, Gove's Chief Luckdragon, calling for 'super-talented weirdos and misfits with odd skills' to apply for new jobs within Number 10.[23]

This sounds right up your Downing Street.

Beating off 35,000 other applicants, including the ones sacked for advocating eugenics and the use of live rounds on BLM protestors, you get the job.

Initially, you revel in the realm of backroom politics.

No voters to worry about. No accountability.

You're one of the Vote Leave lads now. BoJo. Gazza. Caino. Roxstar. The Chatty Rat.

In February you take great delight in forcing the resignation of Sajid Javid.

In March you catch Covid.

In April you offer to drive Dominic Cummings, whose Luckdragon wings have been clipped by the virus, to Barnard Castle to test his eyesight.

In May Michael Gove sacks you both.

You spend the next two years writing enigmatic 3,000-word blog posts, calling Gove a 'complete fuckwit' and comparing your mission to get rid of him to 'fixing the drains'.[24]

In 2022 you release a picture of 'Jon Bon Govi' dancing at a party in the middle of the second lockdown.

Neither of you works in politics again.

The End

25

What's not to like about the Democrats, the party of abortion rights, the three-strikes crime bill and Bill Clinton, the incumbent President whose approach to young damsels in distress is an inspiration to all?

What's more, you've been to both parties' conventions and the Tottymeter is significantly higher at the Democrats'.[25]

In 1996 you decide to challenge Joe Biden, then aged a sprightly 104, in the Democratic Delaware primary for the US Senate.

Anxious to make inroads into his commanding lead in the polls, you invite yourself to address what you believe to be a group of Native Americans.

'*Hè*,' you say, feeling rather pleased with your cultural sensitivity. '*Ndushíinzi Boris. I would like to be your kíhkay.*'

'Why are you speaking a mixture of Munsee and Lenape?' they ask.

'Are you not the Delaware tribe of Indians?' you ask.

'No,' they say. 'We're the Indian-American Business Group of Wilmington.'

'Oh,' you say. 'So where are the Delaware tribe of Indians?'

'They left in 1782.'

'And where are they now?'

'Anadarko, Oklahoma.'

'Where's that?'

'Fifteen hundred miles away.'

'Probably for the best,' you say. 'We're less likely to get scalped.'

Biden beats you in a landslide. You swear a solemn oath to exact your revenge.

Turn to episode 90

26

Like Charles I, Disraeli and Churchill, you are learning a useful heraldic motto to blaze above the crest on your coat of arms: *Numquam excuso, numquam explicare*.

By 2004, however, print journalism is no longer helping your quest for power. You need to find a slot on what Americans call 'television', a Greek-Latin portmanteau word describing the twenty-second content breaks between the commercials.

Donald J. Trump is making waves on *The Apprentice*, a show in which wannabe entrepreneurs compete for the chance to help the host make more money out of his children than he lost in inheritance from his father.

Perhaps a similar show will perform wonders for you?

You alight upon series seven of *The Bachelor*, ABC's reality TV show in which twenty-five fair maidens vie against each other for the conjugal affections of one chivalrous man.

Something about the format makes you think you could be rather good at this. After all, the Knights of the Round Table swore an oath 'to succour any maiden who asks for aid'.

It is one oath you take very seriously indeed.

You apply to go on the show. They accept you, assuming that you are indeed a bachelor.

Unfortunately, you forget to tell your wife first.

This poses a legal – and maybe even a moral – problem in the final elimination round where you are expected to select a wife.

If you decide to select another wife anyway, turn to episode 67

If you own up that you're already married, turn to episode 40

27

Your mature handling of the Pennsylvania Avenue stand-off is widely admired, but in 2022, your third year as US President, the House of Representatives sends its articles of impeachment to the Senate.

Your 'high crimes and misdemeanours' include: changing the rules to prevent elected representatives from lobbying on behalf of businesses with a turnover of less than $10 billion; using your powers under Article II, Section 3 of the Constitution to become the first President to adjourn Congress; employing a minority whip called Mr Fanny-Groper; losing the mid-terms; and holding a party in the White House garden during which two glasses, a swing and a karaoke set get broken.

You're acquitted in the Senate, but you've had enough of America.

Stuffing the Oval Office's bust of Churchill into your hand luggage, you decide to head back to Europe to be Secretary General of NATO.

Turn to episode 91

28

The general election of 2024 is fought along similar lines to the US presidential election the same year. Protestors gassed. Punch-ups on televised debates. And, emerging triumphant in both countries at the end of a long, bloody campaign, an oversized, iconoclastic blond toddler.

You decide to double down on your Trumpian populism.

French fishermen attempt to blockade Jersey. You threaten to nuke Martinique, Réunion and South Kensington.

The SNP seeks another referendum, complaining that Scotland voted overwhelmingly to Remain. You rebuild Hadrian's Wall.

Northern Ireland complains about the backstop. You send in the Paratroopers.

Climate change gremlins glue themselves to the third runway at Heathrow. You run them over with a bulldozer.

In 2025 you finally reap the Brexit benefits by signing an enormous UK–US trade deal. The US sends you 900 million chlorine-washed chickens per year; you send them three Melton Mowbray pork pies and a Cornish pasty.

In 2026, just as President Trump is unsuccessfully impeached for the third time (for using classified government documents, covered in gold paint, as wallpaper in his Mar-a-Lago home), it emerges that you used an Oxford comma *and* a hanging gerund in one of your 'named day' parliamentary questions.

Outraged, your party attempts to remove you in a vote of no confidence.

Triumphant but bruised, you decide it's time to change the rules.

First you amend the constitution of the 1922 Committee to make you immune to internal challenges for another ten years. Then you scrap the BBC's licence fee. A minor fire starts in the basement of the House of Goblins – you declare a state of emergency and blame it on the close links between trade union gremlins and the Labour Party. You push through an 'Enabling Act', giving you greater powers to bypass Parliament. You ban the Labour Party – and all newspapers except the *Daily Mail*. You appoint judges – and contestants on *Strictly* – directly. You make the police – and all presenters on GB News – swear an oath of loyalty directly to you.

On 19 June 2034, your seventieth birthday, you arrive in Trafalgar Square to unveil a new statue.

It commemorates your third year as Childlike

Emperor of Great Britain (but not Northern Ireland, which has voted to join Éire).

Yes, you passed an Act in what remains of the House of Goblins to make this your official title.

Nearly all your wishes have been fulfilled.

Next step, the world.

The great and the good are all here. Jacob Rees-Mogg, Reichskanzler of the Exchequer. Priti Patel, Gauleiter of Rwanda. Nadine Dorries, Minister for Banning the BBC. Liz Truss, Minister for Seeing Which Way the Wind is Blowing.

You all glance up at Nelson's Column.

This new statue is taller – no doubt about it.

You wouldn't have commissioned it otherwise.

You give a three-hour speech in Latin.

The dumb masses cheer dutifully.

The cloth is pulled off the statue.

The sun shines off the tousled, gold-plated head (even though you're now completely bald and weigh only eleven stone).

The sun will always shine off the golden head, for the statue will rotate to face the sun.

It is facing you now. Boris's Column. The father of the British.

Your crowning glory.

Now you are truly the Neverending Tory.

But what is this? The statue is still rotating.

It is getting closer.

Falling . . .

Spiralling . . .
Gathering speed . . .
and heading straight towards you.
That wasn't supposed to happen.
Will Rees-Mogg act as a human shield?
No.

The End

29

Biden's accusation wounds you deeply, like a lance grazing your surprisingly thin armour. What possible similarities are there between two rich, blond, womanizing, privileged, ideologically flexible, verbally dexterous populists who made their names on reality TV?

You retort that Trump displays 'quite stupefying ignorance that makes him frankly unfit to hold the office of President of the United States'.[26]

Your comments don't cut through. When has stupefying ignorance ever been a bar to holding high office?

Biden wins the Democratic nomination.

You spend the rest of your career trying – and failing – to steal his son's laptop.

The End

30

Following the departure of your Luckdragon, you have only two people left to answer to: the *Daily Telegraph*, your 'real boss'; and Carrie, your Princess Xayide.

Carrie's continuing obsession is to help you rule Fantastica for ever.

You are several stone lighter, a shadow of your former self.

Has she put you back on a vegan diet?

Has Covid robbed you of your magic powers?

Or is the fulfilment of your wishes still damaging you, just as Michael Gove feared?

Meanwhile, the *Telegraph*'s obsession is with ending Covid restrictions as soon as possible.

You have some sympathy with this position.

'No more fucking lockdowns – let the bodies pile high in their thousands.'[27]

You deny saying this – although, frankly, you would, wouldn't you?

You eventually do the 'inhuman' thing and cancel Christmas 2020 anyway (apart from the Downing Street Christmas quizzes).

And most of the spring, too (apart from another Downing Street leaving party, the night before the Duke of Edinburgh's funeral).

By the summer of 2021 the *Telegraph* – and your backbench Orcs – are getting quite angsty about all this Covid cancelling, the latest twist in the cancel culture wars.

Can't you just no-platform Covid?

You throw your Orcs some red meat by publishing your roadmap out of lockdown, but then you bait the beast again by pushing 'Freedom Day' back from 21 June to 19 July.

Cases continue to soar.

If you decide to postpone Covid Freedom Day again, turn to episode 78

If you decide to press ahead with Covid Freedom Day, turn to episode 59

31

In 2001 you finally enter the mythical Fantastica of British politics, breaking your promise to Conrad Black by standing for election in Henley.

You bring mirth and merriment (and the first of many book deals) to the campaign stump. According to A. A. Gill, you are 'without doubt the very worst putative politician I've ever seen in action . . . utterly, chronically useless – and I can't think of a higher compliment'.[28]

At one point you eye a baby 'as if it were Sunday lunch'.[29]

Or maybe you're just trying to work out if it's one of yours.

Regardless, the voters of Henley clasp you to their matronly bosoms.

You enter Parliament, that House of Goblins, under the household of Sir William of Fourteen Pints and the Misguided Baseball Cap. Admitted to a mythical palace at last, you wander through the Queen's Robing Room, admiring the paintings and thick woodcarvings detailing the heroic life of King Arthur.

Maybe you chat to fellow newbies as you do so: the dashing knights Sir Dave and Sir Gideon.

However, you're wary of these old companions of the Order of Bullingdon.

Both of them seem to think that the Childlike Empress, who has now moved from the House of Goblins to the Land of Ghosts, a nearby red palace populated by snoring old gnomes, has also bestowed her amulet on them.

So maybe they're neverending Tories too.

In which case you're going to have to end them.

But how?

Their fiefdom is a postcode of North Kensington known to estate agents and political journalists as Notting Hill. Yours is in Islington – or wherever else you lay your head, your sword and your pants of an evening.

And while Sir Dave was neither a King's Scholar nor a member of Pop, you will never forgive him for trumping your 2:1 in Classics with a First in PPE.

One day you will avenge this slur.

Right now, however, it is becoming clear that you lack some of the heroic virtues necessary to succeed in your quest: chastity, courage, faith, fortitude, honesty, humility, loyalty, prudence and reason.

In fact, it is not clear which virtues you do possess.

By 2005, you have apologized to Liverpool, Michael Howard and your second wife.

You have also been sacked by *The Spectator*, Michael Howard – but not yet your second wife.

To prove your short-lived credentials as Shadow Arts Minister, you have written another book, a 'novel' called *Seventy-two Virgins* about an unfaithful, badly dressed, cycling, part-time Tory backbencher.

You are rated 525 out of 659 in terms of attendance in the House of Goblins.[30]

By your own admission, you are 'crap' in the Chamber.[31]

While writing your column for *GQ* you have racked up £4,500 in parking fines[32] (which, legally speaking, are no worse than, say, a Prime Minister receiving a fixed penalty notice for hosting super-spreader Covid parties).

'I am a juggler,' you tell a newspaper interviewer. 'I can have it all.'[33]

You're not a very good juggler (although you are an excellent clown).

You are drifting.

Your quest is in danger.

But after the 2005 general election there is a vacancy for the party leadership.

If you reluctantly support Sir Dave, turn to **episode 16**

If you decide to run yourself, turn to **episode 55**

32

Briefly, you serve simultaneously as Mayor of New York and US Secretary of State. After all, an oath not to hold two jobs at the same time doesn't count if your fingers are crossed behind your back.

President (Hillary) Clinton's hope is that some of Britain's long tradition of diplomacy will rub off on you.

She hadn't reckoned on the Kipling.

You quote him at every opportunity: 'Mandalay' to the Burmese; 'The Ballad of East and West' to the Indians; 'The White Man's Burden' to the Africans.

You charm the other half of the world by referring to their 'watermelon smiles', 'letterbox' burkas and 'tank-topped bumboys'.[34]

You visit Beijing and give President Xi Jinping a painting by George Cruikshank of the First Opium War.

As the overseas figurehead of a country that matters, these actions have consequences.

The press, a 'ravening Hyrcanian tiger deprived of its mortal prey',[35] bays for your blood.

Quoting Kipling back at you – 'The female of the

species is more deadly than the male' – President (Hillary) Clinton suggests that you might want to resign in order to spend more time with your families.

But it is too late. You have already started a nuclear war with Iran after mistakenly labelling innocent American hostages journalists.

You cannot be World King. There is no world left.

The End

33

Deciding that the UK's uncodified constitution is easier to subvert than the USA's, you resolve to become Prime Minister.

First, however, you take your disappointing 2:1 in Classics where everyone takes their disappointing 2:1 in Classics: a management consulting firm.

Here you can use your knowledge of Homer, Ancient Greek history and philology to advise supermarket chains on how to roll out integrated logistics and warehouse distribution IT platforms.

After a week you profess yourself physically unable to 'look at an overhead projection of a growth-profit matrix and stay conscious'.[36]

If you decide to stick at it, turn to episode 53

If it's time for another career, turn to episode 19

34

Most of the polls, a magical divining tool run by the Mythical Mermaids of Ipsos MORI, point towards a victory for Remain. You decide to join the campaign, even though the pro-Remain article 'stuck in your craw to write'.[37]

The Orcs of the Eurosceptic Right are furious. What about The Nothing threatening to swallow them whole? You reply that you've always been pro-EU. In 2001 you supported Ken Clarke for the leadership and in 2003 you told the House of Goblins: 'I am not by any means a Eurosceptic. I am a bit of a fan of the European Union. If we did not have one, we would invent something like it.'[38]

However, you quickly clash with fellow Remainers over the tone of the campaign. You want upbeat boosterism. *Boris Unleashed. Great Britain inside a Great EU.*

Sir Dave and Sir Gideon want Project Fear.

To settle the dispute, you challenge Sir Gideon to a duel in a lift.[39]

If you decide to fight dirty, turn to episode 56

If you stick to Queensberry Rules, turn to episode 86

35

Head bowed and humbled, you head north to Michigan on your 'pilgrimage of penitence'.[40]

You arrive in Detroit, the symbol of the Rust Belt and the third most dangerous city in the United States, driving a brand-new Japanese car and wearing a cheap suit made in China.

You climb out of your car on Woodward Avenue.

A man approaches.

'Do you feel lucky, punk?' he asks.

'Golly gosh gumdrops,' you reply.

He reaches into his pocket.

You reach into yours.

He pulls out a Smith & Wesson 9mm.

You pull out *Aeneid* Book IV.

The only thing that stops a bad guy with a gun is a good guy with a copy of Virgil.

He cocks the gun.

You crouch low, as if preparing to join a bully in bad calx in the Eton Wall Game.

'Wallow in this victimhood,' he says.

'Cripes,' you say.
You are the 386th murder in Detroit this year.

The End

36

Despite your housemaster's fears, in 1983 you go up to Balliol, Oxford, home to Heath (boo), Curzon (hurrah), Denis Healey (double boo) and Asquith's concept of 'effortless superiority' (double hurrah), eager to fall in love and find even more faithful companions to accompany you on your quest.

But who will they be?

Sir Call-Me-Dave Cameron, a tall, handsome knight who will still not dignify the Prosciutto Affair allegation with a response?

Sir George-Don't-Call-Me-Gideon Osborne, another courtly member of the Bullingdon Club, whose amusing culture of pleb-bashing, escort-hiring and restaurant-trashing you will later dismiss as 'toffishness and twittishness'?[41]

Michael Gove, a funny little hobgoblin in a kilt who inhabits a completely different mythical world (of people who didn't go to public school)?

We shall come back to all of them shortly.

Meanwhile, your first of many Guineveres is called Allegra.

What first attracted you to this rich, talented,

popular *Tatler* model who was happy to do all your laundry for you?

We can't be sure. But we do know that you woo her by turning up to her party a day early – perhaps the first time in your life you haven't been late for something.

You arrive, panting, at her rooms in Trinity, where you realize your error.

She is all alone, studying.

There is no wine, no cheese and no vomit on the walls.

This looks more like a work event than a party.

You wonder about making your excuses and leaving.

But she is very beautiful.

And at this point in your life, you're very much pro-Remain.

Turn to episode 85

37

You take the first step on your long journey to becoming American President by studying at Harvard after Oxford.

You like the male bonding and the Greek names of the fraternity clubs. But after a wild party at a house owned by the Delta Omicron Variant, during which you accidentally use someone else's oat milk to top up your herbal tea, your university career is in ruins.

You leave Harvard, you joke, *magna sine laude*.

No one gets the joke.

Undeterred, you use the British charm that made Toby Young so popular in America to blag a job as a reporter on the *New York Times*. Here, like Paul's Ephesians (and Jonathan Aitken), you can put on the full armour of God: the breastplate of righteousness; the sword of truth.

Your first article is about the unlikely discovery of Edward II's palace in downtown Manhattan, including a fabricated quote from your godfather about Edward's relationship there with Piers Gaveston, 'his catamite' who had died a decade before the palace was built.[42]

You are sacked.

Over 200 American newspaper editors sign a petition deploring 'behaviour bringing the noble calling of American journalism into disrepute' – and vowing that you will never again be employed in the media in the USA.

If you decide to try your luck in Washington DC regardless, turn to episode 6

If you return to the UK, turn to episode 33

38

Temporarily forgetting about your quest to defeat The Nothing of Europe, you decide that you will do everything you can to exact your revenge on Jonathan Ross and win your own BAFTA.

You pitch a comedy sketch show with the Conservative Member of Parliament for Sutton Coldfield, called *That Mitchell and Johnson Look*.

You present *QI* – and appear on more book cover puff quotes than Stephen Fry.

You host *The Apprentice*, in which you struggle to fire anyone; *Dragons' Den*, in which you give money to anyone who asks for it (as long as they're not a child in food poverty); and *The Great British Bake Off*, in which you make your cake and have your cake and eat your cake (which is always, *always* oven-ready).

You present an episode of *Grand Designs* in which a struggling couple earning £650,000 a year attempt to build a children's treehouse with bulletproof glass on a budget of less than £150,000.

You are briefly The Stig, *Top Gear*'s tame racing

driver, coaching the stars in the reasonably priced cars. But you can't bear the anonymity of the role. So King BloJo joins Captain Slow, the Hamster and the Orangutan to become one of the show's presenters, engaging in some Top Male Banter while visiting the world's most beautiful countries – and insulting them.

Always reading the runes – as well as ruining the autocue readings – you're one step ahead of the media zeitgeist. You do the early seasons of *Made in Chelsea* and the *X Factor*, moving on to *Love Island* and *Britain's Got Talent* just before the audiences do.

By 2016 you're a National Treasure, like David Attenborough, the Queen and Jack the Ripper.

A million people follow you on Instagram, eager to pick up fashion tips on how to pair Hawaiian shorts with a collared shirt and a bandana while going for a jog.

You flaunt your beach-ready body on TikTok.

You tweet in Latin.

You are the influencers' influencer.

You've forgotten all about the Childlike Empress.

In fact, you've grown quite fond of The Nothing, which keeps paying you European residuals for your TV shows.

But is there something missing (apart from the BAFTA)?

You decide to use your celebrity to campaign for Britain to remain in the EU. But despite your Very Serious Letter co-signed by Jude Law, Keira Knightley and Benedict Cumberbatch, Britain still votes to leave.

If this experience has given you a taste for politics, turn to episode 22

If you decide to steer clear of politics, turn to episode 81

39

The inadequacy of the western withdrawal from the Desert of Shattered Hopes gives Putin, Lord of the Many-Coloured Deaths, the confidence to take a break from his deer-antler-blood baths and invade Ukraine in February 2022.

You are not scared of Putin. After all, you successfully shook off the Russian security services' spell in an enchanted Italian castle in 2018. And you still have the protection of the Childlike Empress's silver amulet.

You're desperate to visit Ukraine personally.

You feel a deep bond with the Ukrainian people – especially with their hugely popular President, a comedian whose political candidacy in 2019 was widely thought a joke.

You also need to get away from a Banshee in Fantastica called Sue Gray, whose imminent report screams political death. Your magical *Sikanda* has temporarily stopped working, your ability to find the right words for the right occasion replaced by you madly muttering 'All guidance was completely followed' again and again.

Maybe a visit to Ukraine will rejuvenate your powers.

In April, the Foreign Office finally relents and you embark on one of your more successful foreign trips.

'Be brave, like Boris,' says the delighted Ukrainian Defence Ministry. 'Be brave, like Ukraine.'

President Zelensky heaps praise on you.

Cometh the hour, cometh the comedians.

Your tri-lingual videos are viewed by millions worldwide.

'*Slava Ukraini,*' you say to the Ukrainian people.[43]

You have found your *Sikanda* again.

It's fun playing at Being an International Statesman.

More fun than contemplating the 126 fixed penalty notices about to be issued by the Met Police.

Maybe you'll stay here.

If you decide to stay in Ukraine, turn to episode 62

If you return home, turn to episode 41

40

Your success on *The Bachelor* turns you into an American TV sensation. Few viewers forget the final scene where you reject both remaining contestants and declare your love for your wife, calling out the deep-rooted patriarchy which you say was your inspiration for infiltrating the show in the first place.

Then you have an affair with the producer.

All romantics, you say, 'need the mortar of cynicism to hold themselves up'.[44]

Your media personality is now well established. You are one of the elite, while simultaneously thumbing your nose at the elites. Life is one big joke – and, for now, you're going to let everyone else in on it.

To continue your quest, you take your brains, geniality, boundless self-confidence, sense of the absurd and on-off relationship with the truth to New York. You quickly secure columns in the *Post* and the *Times*; a wardrobe sourced primarily from Walmart; and a talk show on NBC, which provides an apartment whenever your wife kicks you out.

You're a hit. You're Big Boris in the Big Apple.

You're the Beatles, not the Kinks; Simon Cowell,

not Cheryl Tweedy-Cole-Fernandez-Versini (even if you, too, sometimes need subtitles during your star turns on *The Late Show with Letterman*).

Letterman says: 'People always ask me the same question: "Is Boris a very clever man pretending to be an idiot?" And I always say, "No." '[45]

It takes people a while to work out what this means.

You're now the most popular person in the city. Despite having never held elected office, prosecuted the mafia, invented the Johnson financial computer terminal or felt a stream of hair dye trickling down your face while defending fraudulent claims about fraudulent presidential elections, you wonder about running for Mayor of New York in the 2005 election.

If you decide to run for Mayor of New York, turn to episode 61

If you stick with the lucrative media career, turn to episode 89

41

You return home in the spring of 2022 to the full publication of Sue Gray's report, the resignation of your anti-corruption champion *and* your ethics adviser, boos outside St Paul's at the Queen's Platinum Jubilee (bloody lefty, hand-wringing, snowflake monarchists), two imminent by-elections and a vote of no confidence.

On balance, you preferred being in Ukraine.

So you decide to skip campaigning in the June by-elections and go back to the Swamps of Sadness for a second visit.

After all, your resounding victory in the vote of no confidence means you're completely safe for another year, doesn't it?

Hello, Volodymyr. It's good to see a loyal friend again.

If you decide to stay longer in Ukraine this time, turn to episode 62

If you return home again, turn to episode 84

42

You're going to sleep in Downing Street, of course.

You just need to give Theresa May a few more months to bleed out from a thousand cuts: a no-confidence vote, fifth place in the European elections, and a bad cough (before you could blame it on Covid).

In the meantime, you venture to Camberwell, in the Badlands south of the Silver River, to sleep with a fair maiden twenty-four years younger than you.

Another wish come true.

Your future third wife has many sexist nicknames.

Lady Macbeth.

Carrie Antoinette.

Cersei from *Game of Thrones*.

Princess Nut Nut.

And a few others which, for legal reasons, are best looked up on Twitter (but not in *The Times*).[46]

Your supporters' biggest fear, however, is that she'll be your Princess Xayide, the sorceress who speaks of a new Fantastica where you, 'the Great Knower', will take all the power that is rightfully yours; where you reign unscrutinized and untouchable for ever; where you finally become the Childlike Emperor.

It's not all a middle-aged man's fantasy, however.

Carrie persuades you to cut your hair. And to try a new diet of magical plants from the forest.

You are briefly full of beans.

But in 2019, just as you're fighting the Conservative leadership battle, one of your arguments becomes so heated that your Camberwell neighbours call the *Guardian* (and the police).

Will this derail your leadership bid?

Of course not. You're up against Jeremy Hunt.

On 24 July 2019 you are finally handed the mythical key (there is no lock; there is no key) to Number 10 that has driven your quest for so long. Facing a ticking Brexit timeline and a mutinous House of Goblins, you walk proudly into Downing Street with a pregnant sorceress in order to live with Michael Gove's Luckdragon, Dominic 'the career psychopath' Cummings.[47]

What could possibly go wrong?

Turn to episode 75

43

Oh dear. You've just started a civil war that lasts several decades, pitting young against old, north against south, and ripping entire families apart.

Perhaps you know what that feels like.

The End

44

In September 2023 you initiate a successful vote of no confidence in the leadership of Liz Truss.

In 2024 you win a landslide election on the promise of taking Britain back into the EU.

The Childlike Empress howls like a Banshee in her grave when, in 2031, you become the most popular EU Commissioner since Peter Mandelson and Jean-Claude Juncker.

But you don't need her any more.

You are a slave to The Nothing.

You are World King (European Division).

The End

45

What's not to like about the Republicans, the party of Reaganomics, chastity and the belief that homosexuality is incompatible with military service?

You admire Reagan because he admired Thatcher, the Childlike Empress who continues to control the Fantastica of Britain – even though you still haven't met her yourself.

You claim that you were 'never one of those acnoid Tory boys who had semi-erotic dreams about her visiting you at night in her imperial-blue dress and bling and magnificent pineapple-coloured hair ... leaning over and parting her red lips to whisper about monetarism and taming union power'.[48]

You seem to have given this dream – which you definitely didn't have – quite a lot of thought.

Bob Dole is your Republican presidential candidate in 1996. Like Julius Caesar, Elmo from *Sesame Street* and toddlers everywhere, he has the unusual habit of referring to himself in the third person.

Alexander Boris Caesar de Pfeffel Elmo Johnson, fledgling World King and eternal toddler, admires this use of illeism.

But you're not running for the White House yet. Most political careers start – as well as end – with failure. And right now you're in a town hall in Charleston struggling in the West Virginia Senatorial primary.

'Can you tell us about your faith?' asks a man in the audience.

A bead of sweat trickles down your collar.

'I believe that voting Republican will cause your wife to have bigger breasts and increase your chances of owning a BMW M3,' you answer.[49]

'I don't *believe* that was the question,' says the moderator.

'Oh, my *faith*?' you say. 'Well, it's a bit like Magic FM in the Chilterns. The signal comes and goes.'[50]

'What?' says the moderator.

'WHAT?' says the angry audience. 'IT COMES AND GOES?'

Your opponent senses blood.

'Boris subscribes to a pre-Christian morality system with a multitude of gods and no clear set of rules,' he says.[51]

'Gods bless America,' you try to quip – but it is too late. The audience is already pulling out .380-calibre semiautomatic pistols. Sawn-off shotguns. Well-thumbed copies of the Old Testament.

You fought West Virginia – but West Virginia is fighting back.

You eye up the fire escape.

Less Knight of the Round Table. More Brave Sir Robin.

Venisti, vidisti, fugisti.

You came, you saw, you ran away.

Your ass is peppered with shot the whole way from Charleston to Washington Dulles International.

The End

46

What a party pooper!

How would you know if this event was against the rules which you set?

Your gnomes boo as they wobble back to work, one of them giving your son's swing a vicious kick for good measure, another performing an essential press-up to point out the absurdity of the rules.

You feel awful. It's so tough on them, coming into their meaningful, well-paid jobs while sending their children to key-worker schools.

And it's so tough on you, not being loved by everyone.

Maybe you'll relent next time.

Turn to episode 69

47

Now that you are Mayor of London, you can wield
Sikanda, your magical *Telegraph* column, again. Your
weekly contribution of 1,100 words provides some
useful 'chickenfeed'[52] of £250,000 on top of your
bantam-feed mayoral salary of £137,579.

This little extra will be helpful for feeding another
chicken, hatched from a different hen in 2009.
According to the editor of the *Daily Mail*, the nation's
all-seeing, all-knowing moral guardian, you have the
'morals of an alley cat'.[53]

You spend ten hours a month writing your
column – slightly less than you spend being Mayor.

Somehow, though, you turn out to be rather good
at the job, delegating the parts you don't like, such as
discussing detailed policy, and focusing on the bits
you do like, such as overspending on building projects and making jokes about the 'Glass Gonad' of
City Hall, your imperial Ivory Tower office perched
on its 'upper epidermis . . . somewhere near the sem-
inal vesicle'.[54]

You are more popular after a year than you were
when you started. A poll reveals that over 70 per cent

of women *and* men would be interested in having sex with you.

This feeling is probably mutual.

You discover many other advantages to being the most senior elected Tory in the country. You can sack someone called Blair (even if he's only Chief Commissioner of the Met). You can snipe at Gordon Brown. And best of all, you can lob bricks at Sir Dave, the party leader.

'Piffle,' you label his flagship policy, the Big Society.[55]

'It's all gone tits up – call for Boris,' tweets Rachel, your sister, after the Conservatives fail to win a majority in the general election in 2010.[56]

If you answer her call, turn to episode 71

If you ignore her, turn to episode 63

48

'What are you doing?' asks your Luckdragon, Dominic Cummings.

You stop jumping up and down on the broad-brimmed straw hat typically worn in Mexico and throw it across the Cabinet Room.

'I'm trying to squash the sombrero,' you say.

'I think we're going to need a more effective Covid strategy,' says Cummings.

What? More effective than herd immunity? More effective than watching racing at Cheltenham, rugby at Twickenham – and missing five COBRA meetings?

Yes, he says.

Golly.

Maybe you should get Professor Chris Whitty, the Chief Alchemist, to inject you with Covid live on TV to show everyone that it's nothing to be scared of?[57]

No, says Cummings.

If you decide to do it anyway, turn to episode 15

If you listen to your Luckdragon, turn to episode 57

49

Now this is your sort of party. A restored Italian palazzo with breathtaking views over the Umbrian countryside. Glamour models. 'Nothing off the menu'.[58]

There's also a former KGB officer turned oligarch ogre with close ties to Putin, Lord of the Many-Coloured Deaths.

You meet the KGB officer.

Four years later you finally admit this: 'As far as I am aware, no government business was discussed.'[59]

According to eyewitnesses at San Francesco d'Assisi airport the day after the party, you probably weren't 'aware' of very much at all. You look like you 'slept in your clothes', you're 'struggling to walk in a straight line' and you appear to be on the verge of being 'sick on the tarmac'.[60]

Apart from a 'thick book about war strategy', you appear to have no luggage.

But you do have some vague memories of being

placed under a spell and recruited as a Russian sleeper agent.

If you think you said yes, turn to episode 5

If you're sure you said no, turn to episode 66

50

Tobias Ellwood, chair of the Defence Select Committee, thinks you have 'more chance of becoming a Bond villain than being head of NATO'.[61]

Which killjoy said you can't be both?

In May 2023 you go to NATO's headquarters in Brussels to test the waters.

You haven't been here since defeating The Nothing. Who knows what strange monsters you'll awaken?

But then something very odd indeed happens.

You travel freely around the continent, crossing borders without waiting in six-hour queues.

You order goods online without being hit with huge delays and additional VAT.

You find an attractive Dutch au pair who can legally come and live with your family in London.

All this leads to a magical Brusselian Conversion.

Perhaps, you realize, The Nothing is on to Something after all.

So when President Macron vetoes your candidacy to become NATO Secretary General, you see it as a blessing in disguise.

You return, energized, to Britain and campaign vigorously to rejoin the EU under Article 49.

There is nothing (half) the country likes more than an erring sinner – especially with EU inflation running at a manageable 12 per cent compared to Weimar Britain's 82 per cent.

You're even courted by the Lib Dems and Labour, inspired by the zeal of the converted.

Seeing which way the wind is blowing, One Nation Tory goblins cluster round their prodigal son, finding you a safe seat in the Home Counties.

By the summer you're being spoken of as a serious challenger for Downing Street.

Turn to episode 44

51

It is 2014 and you are sitting in your mayoral office in the Glass Gonad reading the reviews of your latest ~~job application~~ book, *The Churchill Factor: How One Man Made History*.

> *'. . . like being cornered in the Drone Club and harangued for hours by Bertie Wooster . . .'*[62]

> *'The reader is invited to see the two men as supreme orators, literary masters and slayers of spineless Conservatives and perfidious foreigners.'*[63]

> *'With more than an eye on the battle to succeed David Cameron, and to keep Nigel Farage at bay, Johnson equates the European Union, time and again, with the crushing of the British spirit.'*[64]

> *'He refers to himself some thirty times in the short introduction alone.'*[65]

You smile to yourself. A job well done.

You put your hand where your heart used to be, feeling the Childlike Empress's silver amulet nestled against your skin. Last April, she went to live in a Cloud Palace in the sky, serenaded by dwarves playing lutes and the BBC playing the chart hit from 1939 'Ding Dong the Witch is Dead'.

You miss her. But she is still with you. Your wishes are still coming true.

And now she's gone, there's a vacancy at last in Fantastica.

A hobgoblin knocks at the door.

It is Michael Gove.

He has spent the last four years trying unsuccessfully to fight a terrifying mythical creature, made up of innumerable small, buzzing insects that can shape-shift, inflicting deadly wounds with its venomous sting. It is known as 'The Many' or 'The Blob'.

Michael Gove is no longer the Secretary of State for Education.

But watch out: he would still like to be a Neverending Tory.

'What do those pins represent?' he asks, innocently, gesturing at the large map of southern England behind your desk.

You swivel round and scratch your head. What *do* they represent? Is it where your children live? Your mistresses? Your debtors?

Suddenly it comes back to you.

'They're potential constituencies at the next general election,' you say.

'But you've repeatedly denied that you would serve as an MP while mayor,' says Gove.

You give him a long, hard stare of total in-comprehension.

Sir Dave is unpopular; Sir Gideon more so. You've survived a bruising interview with Eddie Mair in which he called you a 'nasty piece of work'.[66] And, most interestingly, a recent poll suggests that 83 per cent of Tory members want a referendum on EU membership – and 70 per cent would vote to Leave before The Nothing swallows them whole.

Of course you're going back to the House of Goblins.

Time to look up Uxbridge and South Ruislip on Wikipedia.

Turn to episode 4

52

'Alexander! Alexander!'

Your mother is calling you.

It's time for your favourite story, the *Iliad for Infants.*

'Little Al! Little Al!'

Where is she?

'ALEXANDER JOHNSON!'

She's cross now.

But so are you. Alexander Johnson? It's such a banal name. So *normal.* How are you meant to make your way in the world with a name like that?

Al Gore. Alexander Hamilton. Alexander the Great. Alexander Kerensky. Danny Alexander.

Losers, one and all.

You might as well be called Keir.

The End

53

Despite your unpromising start in the world of management consultancy, you turn out to be rather good at it. The three key skills, it seems, are:

Telling people what they want to hear.

Making recommendations – and not worrying too much about whether anyone implements them.

Inventing very large numbers.

After a few years, you take your wife and your first four children to Dubai, where the rulers allow you to acquire three more Junior Wives and twelve more children.

Dubai is booming, and you are given free rein to boom it further. The world's largest shopping mall. The world's tallest tower. The world's most-resembling-a-giant-phallus hotel.

If your five-year-old self playing with the Lego set could see you now!

World Sheikh Boris is in seventh heaven.

But then you make a joke someone dislikes.

You're thrown into a squalid Dubai jail for forty-five years.

The British Foreign Secretary decides to leave you to rot.

The End

54

You graciously acknowledge the melodrama through which you've dragged the country and your party by standing outside Downing Street on 7 July 2022 and saying how sorry you feel for yourself.

As you said to a reunion of Pop, Eton's prefect body, in 2011: 'Never apologize to the ordinary members of the school.'[67]

The *Daily Mail* publishes a commemorative fiction edition, praising you for standing down with your 'dignity and reputation intact'.[68]

Give that editor-in-chief a peerage (if not the chairmanship of Ofcom).

You tease the House of Goblins with a final 'Hasta la vista, baby' (which is not the first time you've said goodbye to a baby).

Yes, that's right: the Neverending Tory will be back.

This, one might say, is only the end of the beginning.

And now your summer of fun can start.

A lavish wedding at the Cotswold estate of a Tory donor.

A trip in a typhoon fighter jet.

A holiday in Slovenia.

Another in Greece.

More wishes fulfilled.

More COBRA meetings missed.

It's great being a caretaker Prime Minister!

But then the reality of September hits. The removal vans are outside. Liz Truss, the 'Iron Weathercock',[69] is on her way to see the Queen. Princess Xayide has removed the final strip of Lulu wallpaper with her fingernails.

You're a 'booster rocket that has fulfilled its function'.[70]

What on earth are you going to do next?

If you stay in the House of Commons for now, turn to episode 87

If you decide to resign as an MP, turn to episode 65

55

In 2005 you decide that your extensive political experience – four years popping in and out of the House of Goblins, a few million words of dashed-off journalese, and the Presidency of the Oxford Union in 1986 – makes you the ideal candidate to be the fifth Tory leader walked all over by Tony Blair.

Somehow the Conservative Party membership agrees with you. You wow the old goat-men of the Tory party by speaking for fifteen whole minutes at the autumn conference without notes, slander or insult. Among MPs, the Right's vote is split between David Davis and Liam Fox; the Left's between Sir Dave and Ken Clarke.

You reach the final round of voting alongside Davis. The old goat-men, tickled by your irreverent charm, make you Leader of Her Majesty's Most Loyal Opposition with a thumping majority.

Unfortunately, they've made a grave mistake.

Sir Dave, whom you appoint Shadow Secretary of State for the Environment, urges you to 'detoxify the brand'. You disagree. There is nothing wrong with the Conservative brand. You launch your draconian crime policy with an invitation to the public to 'slug a hoodie'. You discard the party's torch icon – and replace it with a heraldic crest of two snakes biting each other's tails and the motto 'Floreat Etona'.

You dispatch Sir Dave to the Arctic Circle to shoot some huskies.

An interviewer from the *Southern Oracle* asks if you've ever taken drugs.

'I had a normal university experience,' you reply.

What do you mean by that, you're asked.

Dope, cocaine, white-tie parties and smashed-up restaurants, you reply.

You briefly soar in the polls.

You announce all-women shortlists – and offer to interview every female parliamentary candidate yourself.

You back Sir Gideon to be Mayor of London in 2008 – and you're delighted when he loses to a five-headed newt gremlin called Livingstone.

Asked if you'd ever go into coalition with the Liberal Democrats, you liken Nick Clegg to a 'cut-price edition of David Cameron hastily knocked off by a Shanghai sweatshop to satisfy market demand'.[71]

All the signs point to you defeating Gordon Brown in a landslide at the next election.

But then in 2009, the *Daily Telegraph* reveals the MPs' expenses scandal. It turns out that you have single-handedly billed the taxpayer over £1 million for duck houses, bathplugs, moat cleaning, council tax, second-home mortgage flipping and a drinks trolley worth £3,675.

Following the 2010 general election, Gordon Brown goes into coalition with the Liberal Democrats, introducing proportional representation, a mansion tax and tuition fees before handing over to a benevolent elf called David Miliband.

Following the 2010 general election, you go to jail.

Them's the breaks.

The End

56

After experiencing the most painful wedgie since the bollock-burner inflicted by Fotherington Minor at St Paul's in 1986, Sir Gideon and Sir Dave reluctantly agree that you can unleash 'Project Cheer' on the electorate in the 2016 referendum.

You commission a red bus emblazoned with the British and EU flags and the slogan: 'The EU sends us £86 million a week in regional aid and farm subsidies. Let's keep Britain Great.'

You drive the bus all over the country (Amber Rudd even lets you drive her home at night), extolling the benefits of membership. The EU gives us wonderful access to French girls, you say. Spanish beaches. Italian food. German cars.

You help the *Sun* secure a royal scoop with the headline 'Queen Backs Remain'.

You rip Rees-Mogg a new one when he says that Louis XIV, Napoleon and Hitler 'were all trying to create a United States of Europe'.[72]

You persuade President Obama to say that Britain will be 'at the front of the queue' in any trade deals – and don't mention his 'part-Kenyan' heritage when he does so.[73]

You send the Marine Policing Unit to break up the Thames battle between Nigel Farage and Bob Geldof with some of the water cannons you bought after the London riots (and which Theresa May refused to license).

You ban both Farage and Geldof from speaking in public for ten years.

After Remain win by a landslide, a rejuvenated Sir Dave fulfils his promise to make you Foreign Secretary.

Following your first gaffe – a limerick about the Turkish President having sex with a goat[74] – he sacks you.

Turn to episode 73

57

A bright light appears over the Lonely Mountain.

'What is that?' you ask your Chief Alchemist.

'It is The Science,' he says reverentially.

You decide to follow it (if not the guidance), but The Science leads you to some very strange places.

A lockdown commute to and from Chequers.

A blind eye to Cummings's dash for Durham.

A world-beating number of deaths in the first few months.

The intensive care unit of St Thomas' Hospital.

Briefly, you wonder about emulating your hero Pericles, who died of a plague that swept Ancient Greece. But like the Childlike Empress, you fight on; you fight to win.

Having pulled through, you address the nation on the television.

'~~The NHS is~~ I am the beating heart of this country. ~~It is~~ I am unconquerable. ~~It is~~ I am powered by love.'

Your approval ratings shoot up from 46 per cent to 66 per cent overnight.

Another wish from your silver amulet two-thirds fulfilled.

Soon you might be able to subvert the uncodified constitution and rule Fantastica for ever.

But what will you do now with this new-found popularity?

An eye-wateringly wasteful £37 billion test and trace system that fails to achieve its main objective?

Tick.

A £208,104 refurbishment of your rundown Downing Street hobbit-hole, surreptitiously billed to the Conservative Party?

Absolutely.

A celebratory work event or two (or seventeen) during lockdown?

Let's think about that last one a bit more.

It's a warm evening in May 2020. Your government's Twitter account has just reminded everyone of the latest draconian Covid rules. You wander into the Downing Street garden, where gnomish staffers have spontaneously planned an unplanned work event by spending a week working out how to smuggle bottles of wine past a press conference.

If you decide to send everyone back inside, turn to episode 46

If you implicitly believe this is a work event, turn to episode 69

58

You enter the presidential race in 2020 with a pledge (which no one understands) to steer the country 'between the Scylla and Charybdis'[75] of Bernie Sanders and Donald Trump. During the Democratic Party primaries, Senator Joe Biden, a sprightly 128, describes you as a 'physical and emotional clone' of Trump.[76]

If you disagree with Biden, turn to episode 29

If you agree with him, turn to episode 77

59

For once, your decision to press on with Covid Freedom Day appears to be the correct one, giving you something to bang on about at PMQs for the next year, instead of answering the question.

Cases fall rapidly, allowing you time to focus on more important matters, such as how to evacuate 150 dogs, cats, donkeys (and 15,000 people) from Afghanistan, the Desert of Shattered Hopes.

Operation Save Big Dogs, you might call it.

It's the summer of 2021 and everyone is on holiday – although eyewitness reports that Dominic Raab is paddleboarding in Crete while Kabul falls can't be true as the 'sea is closed'.[77]

You're going to have to make this big call yourself – with a little help from Carrie, your Princess Xayide.

If you decide to rescue the dogs yourself,
turn to episode 80

If you let Kabul fall, turn to episode 39

60

Agreeing with your sister that Michael Gove is 'a political psychopath run by his wife',[78] you decide to get your immediate revenge by fighting him for the party leadership – and the keys to Number 10 – in the summer of 2016.

After three rounds of voting by Tory goblins, it's just Theresa May, Andrea Leadsom and you left.

A *Times* interviewer quotes Leadsom, who has three children, suggesting that motherhood gives her a better political perspective than May, who has none.

You suggest that if the value of a Prime Minister can be judged by how many children they have, you're the perfect candidate.

Leadsom withdraws from the race, leaving you and May to woo the old goat-men of the Tory membership. Faced with a Brexiteer who makes jokes and a Remainer who doesn't, they vote convincingly for you.

Your first PMQs is a triumph. Tearing into Jeremy Corbyn, you reach your peroration by leaning menacingly towards the Leader of the Opposition and lisping, in a basso Churchillian profundo, 'Remind him of anybody?'[79]

A handful of backbench Orcs faint in delight.

But then it all goes horribly wrong.

You're unable to say the phrase 'Hard Brexit' without sniggering.

You start another affair, which is more difficult to keep secret in Downing Street.

Your wife moves out.

You struggle with the domestic burdens of doing the 'boy jobs', like taking out the bins, as well as the 'girl jobs', like running the country.

Your mistress moves in.

While rambling through the Silver Mountains of Snowdonia in 2017, you decide to call a snap election to burnish your 'strong and stable' credentials. You decline to answer a question about the naughtiest thing you've ever done. You lose your majority and go into a weak and wobbly coalition with the Northern Irish Orcs.

Desperate to regain your authority with your mutinous goblins, you dad-dance on to the stage at the 2018 party conference, knocking over the lectern, the Home Secretary and two cameramen.

A prankster hands you a P45, saying, 'Theresa asked me to give this to you.'

You survive a confidence vote, but not the

eventual unveiling of your Brexit deal, which your own Foreign Secretary calls 'a big turd which has emerged zombie-like from the coffin'.[80]

After a record number of ministerial resignations and parliamentary defeats, Michael Gove becomes Prime Minister in 2019.

Turn to episode 24

61

Drawing upon your diverse, 'one-man melting pot' lineage[81] – Christian, Jewish and Muslim – your 2005 campaign for the Mayor of New York is the perfect pitch for a cosmopolitan city still ravaged by 9/11.

You quickly make your mark as Mayor, inventing the Boris Bagel and banning bendy buses, 'the jack-knifing, traffic-blocking, self-combusting, cyclist-crushing, eighteen-metre-long socialist Frankfurters'.[82]

You build a cable car across the Hudson, which no one goes on, and start a bike hire scheme sponsored by Bloomberg L.P.

Everyone calls them Boris Bikes.

Give me another $50 million, you say, and I'll change my name to Bloomberg.

People often stop you in the street to shake your hand. Or to call you a fat prick.

Your greatest triumph, however, comes on the campaign trail in 2005. Conscious that London is the front-runner among the cities shortlisted for the 2012 Olympic Games, you decide that New York needs a high-profile stunt. Heading to the South Bronx, in order to publicize the Olympic velodrome, you launch yourself high above St Mary's Park on a zipwire.

Halfway across you get stuck. Pulling out a Union Jack, you explain: 'This is the sort of disaster you can expect if the Olympics are awarded to a city run by Ken Livingstone.'

The 2012 Summer Olympics and Paralympics are awarded to New York City.

Turn to episode 17

62

Your trip to Ukraine is going so well that you decide to visit the street named after you in Odesa, near the Swamps of Sadness.

This city, known for its famous writers, sandy beaches and hedonistic nightclub scene, sounds right up your вулиця – even if the newly renamed Boris Johnson вулиця is a single-track country metaphor full of potholes and overgrown bushes.

You head south from Kyiv in an armed convoy. Far better to brave the untargeted Russian howitzers than the laser-accurate barbs of David Davis quoting Leo Amery quoting Oliver Cromwell at home.

Like Churchill after Gallipoli in the First World War, you will venture directly into the trenches.

Unfortunately, like Churchill during the Second Boer War, you are captured.

And unlike Churchill, you don't manage to escape.

Perhaps your faux-deprecating admission that you have 'more in common with a three-toed sloth than with Winston Churchill' is true after all.[83]

Putin, Lord of the Many-Coloured Deaths, puts you on trial as a 'terrorist' and 'foreign mercenary'.

You spend the rest of your life in a dungeon in the Swamps of Sadness listening to Pussy Riot on loop.

The End

63

Although he is fatally weakened by the 2010 election, you pledge your full support to Sir Dave, right up to the moment when he no longer has your full support.

Being Mayor in your second term, you discover, is even more fun than in your first term.

2012 is a particularly vintage year.

You meet your future third wife during the campaign.

You defy all forms of political gravity by getting stuck on a zipwire – and becoming even more popular.

Sir Dave attracts widespread derision for leaving one of his children in the pub (although it could be said that you don't always remember to take your children home with you either).

Crowds of loyal dwarves chant your name at the 'ruthlessly and dazzlingly elitist' London Olympics, where 'semi-naked women, glistening like wet otters' play beach volleyball in Horse Guards Parade.[84]

The same crowds boo Sir Gideon of Austerity.

A poll shows that the Tories would only win the next election if you were leader.

You celebrate the opening night of the Paralympics by popping off for an affair in Shoreditch.

You spend the first of many weekends at an enchanted Italian castle owned by the son of a KGB agent.

And so you have reached Peak Boris.

Or have you?

After the Olympics you write: 'It may not get any better than this, but this is good enough for me.'[85]

Or is it?

If you decide to call it a day here, turn to episode 92

If you decide to press on with your quest, turn to episode 51

64

You are now five years old. Well done.

You are at the family's farm in Nethercote, in the happy shire of Somerset, playing, alone, with Lego, when Rachel comes into the room.

'What are you doing, Al?' she asks.

You are playing one of your favourite games. It is called Building Massive, Unfunded Infrastructure Projects to Distract from the Trouble You're In. Earlier this morning you wrote your earliest surviving article, 'Boo to grown-ups!', on the kitchen wall.[86]

It is a mantra that will serve you well into your sixth decade.

'Build, build, build,' you chant as you pile high the Lego bricks, modelling the world in which you will be king. There are police stations, water-cannon factories, bike-docking stations, food banks and forty brand-new hospitals.

'But there were already thirty-seven hospitals on the playroom floor yesterday,' says Rachel. She picks up a discarded piece of Lego. 'And what's this?'

'That's Alexander Airport,' you declare proudly. 'It will be served by Alexander Articulated Lorries laden with Alexander Automobiles crossing via the Alexander Aqueduct to the runways on Alexander Atoll.'

Rachel gives you a withering look, smashing a plump toddler's fist on to a world as unstable as the idea of building a £335 billion bridge across the Irish Sea.

You blink back the tears, surveying your shattered infrastructure dreams.

How are you going to level up now?

If you decide to raise the Alexander Alarm by running to Mummy, turn to episode 52

If you choose to throw a Boris Brick at your sister, turn to episode 13

65

Inspired by Tony Blair and David Cameron, you have no intention of hanging around the pointless House of Goblins a minute longer than is necessary (especially if the Privileges Committee ignores the All-Seeing, All-Knowing Right-Wing Media and does its job properly).

But you're not particularly interested in bringing peace to a Middle East bombed to smithereens or giving PR advice to the dictator of Kazakhstan or opening a methanol factory in Azerbaijan or growing a lockdown mullet or buying a shepherd's hut or sending text messages to Cabinet ministers on behalf of collapsing finance companies.

You still have the Childlike Empress's amulet. Is it too much to wish just to be loved again?

A TV producer calls. They've seen the leaked video of your first dance at your third wedding, grooving to 'Sweet Caroline' like Carrie's sweaty uncle. Would you like to appear on the next season of *Strictly*?

If you say yes, turn to episode 23

If you say no, turn to episode 18

66

There have been three great fellowships in the last 2,000 years: the table of Jesus Christ and his disciples; the table of the Holy Grail, when Joseph of Arimathea brought Christianity to Britain; and the dinner party table of Jacob Rees-Mogg's £5 million house in Queen Anne's Gate where he rallied the Orcs of the European Research Group against Theresa May's compromise Brexit deal.

After her initial absence on the European quest, May is desperate to assert herself as the one true goblin who can unravel the riddle of whether Brexit means Brexit.

But she's not as desperate as you are to get rid of her and become Prime Minister yourself.

She is only a Childlike Empress impersonator. You're the real deal.

Still, you're not sure what to do about her deal at first. You've just about recovered from your Perugia hangover when she invites the Cabinet to Chequers in July 2018 to endorse it.

David Davis resigns and Rees-Mogg is tipped as the next Prime Minister. 'Your death warrant if you sign up and don't resign,' texts Iain Duncan Smith.[87]

'A Chamberlain when we wanted a Churchill,' whisper the cunning Orcs of the ERG.[88]

You're not going to take that lying down.

You resign too.

And for once, it seems that you might be down *and* out.

May gives you the worst office in Parliament.

One of her gofers gives the *Southern Oracle* a 4,000-word dossier on your private life.[89]

Your wife discovers your latest affair and finally boots you out of the family home.

The Permanent Undersecretary gives you forty-eight hours to leave the Foreign Secretary's £20 million grace-and-favour flat. It takes another three weeks (and four more letters from the Permanent Undersecretary) for you to understand that Leave means Leave.

Homelessness has almost trebled under the Tories. It's now almost trebled plus one.

So where are you going to sleep?

If you decide to sleep in your car, turn to episode 21

If you look for another solution, turn to episode 42

67

With some reluctance, you move with your two wives to Salt Lake City where you join the Church of Jesus Christ of Latter Day Saints. It is only later that you discover that the practice of polygamy was actually outlawed by the Church in 1904.

What's the point, you wonder, of being a conservative if you can't turn the clock back to 1904?[90]

You decide to live out the rest of your life in Utah, campaigning for a reinterpretation of Jacob 2:27-30 in the Book of Mormon, so that you can take on a couple more wives.

You end up with fifteen.

You are very happy.

The End

68

You lead the Liberal Democrats through the tumultuous political events of 2019, making little impact in the polls as Prime Minister Gove slugs it out with Jeremy Corbyn.

In the general election in December, you lose your seat.

You decide to give up on politics and return to showbiz. But is your star on the wane?

Turn to episode 23

69

It's your birthday. Happy Work Event to You.

Carrie and her interior designer are upstairs sprinkling hundreds of thousands of pounds of faerie dust over your hobbit-hole.

Suddenly, you're 'ambushed' with a cake in the Cabinet Room.[91]

You are in mortal danger.

How are you going to get out of this one?

Ask them to leave and return one at a time?

Get them to sing 'Happy Birthday' twice while pointlessly washing their hands?

Claim that you stayed for only ten minutes, even though there's nothing in the rules about that?

Remind them of all the children who've missed out on birthday celebrations this year?

Hang on. Who's that? It's an innocent young elf called Rishi. Who invited him? Oh, he's just early for a meeting. Perfect. Here, Rishi, have a slice.

'Pig out to help out', to coin a phrase.

The sweet taste of blackmail.

Turn to episode 8

70

Bong.

It's 11 p.m. on 31 January 2020.

Bong.

You're celebrating Brexit Freedom Day.

Bong.

The best of Britain is on display.

Bong.

Richard Tice, one of the 'Bad Boys of Brexit', is addressing a rally in Trafalgar Square. 'Shine a Light for Europe' protests are taking place across the country. Sadiq Khan's Glass Gonad is offering emotional support and free legal advice for worried EU Londoners.

Bong.

There has also been an aborted crowdfunder to 'bung a bob for a Big Ben Bong'.

Bong.

So ultimately these bongs are another fantasy in your head.

Bong.

Like the notion of Brexit Actually Being Done.

Bong.

Because the Big Ben plan you referred to on *BBC Breakfast* to make the clock chime despite the ongoing renovations didn't actually exist.

Bong.

You squint out of the window, blinking in the glare of the giant substitute clock face projected on to Downing Street.

Bong.

You gag a little on the English food and drink you've ordered for the evening's entertainment. A lukewarm sausage roll from a motorway service station. Jellied eels. Eton Mess.

Bong.

Britain has left the EU. The Nothing has been defeated. But what do you have to put in its place?

Nothing?

Really?

Has it all been a terrible mistake?

No time to think about that now. There's another crisis just round the corner.

Turn to episode 48

71

'Sir Dave,' you say, 'it's all gone tits up. Your Notting Hill-focused, Samantha-inspired, gay marriage-loving, wind turbine-fetishizing, hoody-hugging, husky-bothering, Brussels-buggering, Nothing-nobbing policies have ended you up in bed with "I agree with Nick". It's time for a proper Neverending Tory, the true heir to the Childlike Empress, to take over. I'm challenging you for the leadership.'

'Boris,' says Sir Dave. 'You're no longer an MP.'

'Oh,' you say.

Turn to episode 63

72

Good call. Who says you need a cause anyway – especially a controversial one. Your quest, for now, is to find a quest.

You can see which way the wind is blowing later.

And then piss into it.

For the time being, you're content to be a journalist, not a politician; a spectator, not a player; a kicker-over of sandcastles, not a builder.

Or are you?

After all, no one puts up statues to journalists.

You're going to have to go into politics.

But which party will you join?

If you decide to join the Republicans, turn to episode 45

If you decide to join the Democrats, turn to episode 25

73

You continue to make trouble for Sir Dave from the backbenches despite being sacked as Foreign Secretary, telling everyone that he only won the EU referendum because of you.

Meanwhile, The Nothing of Europe continues to threaten the Fantastica of Great Britain with its terrifying attempts to promote peace, prosperity and the well-being of its citizens.

The defeated Eurosceptics are more vocal than ever.

After UKIP win the European Parliament elections in 2019, you begin to wonder if you backed the wrong side in the referendum.

Is the Childlike Empress punishing you?

You court the Orcs in the European Research Group and the All-Seeing, All-Knowing Right-Wing Media. By 2020 you're too powerful to ignore. Sir Dave reappoints you to the Cabinet, as Secretary of State for Health.

Then a terrible plague sweeps the world.

You've got this.

You have a mate in the pub with some spare PPE equipment.

You break social distancing rules with a co-worker, the two of you caught in a 'steamy clinch' by the *Southern Oracle*.

You throw your magical, protective ring around care homes by discharging patients with Covid to die there.

Sir Dave keeps you in post because you're a useful scapegoat for the government's failures when the inevitable inquiry starts.

But then in 2021 you pull off a masterstroke, falsely claiming that Fantastica's rapid vaccine roll-out owes its success to your deliberate breaching of regulation 174 of the EU's Human Medicine Regulations 2012.

Imagine what else Britain could do if she ignored other EU regulations which she is already allowed to ignore, you argue.

This argument goes down a storm with the Eurosceptic Orcs.

'Defeat The Nothing!' they chant.

You can feel the force of the Childlike Empress again.

Taking a leaf out of Nicola Sturgeon's book, you propose that the next once-in-a-generation referendum on EU membership should be held in a third-of-a-generation's time, in 2023.

You lead the Leave campaign to a stunning victory and become Prime Minister in 2024.

Turn to episode 28

74

That's right: you *can* have your cake and eat it – again. You can listen to Lynton *and* let Boris be Boris.

But who is Boris in 2008?

Let's have a look in the Magic Mirror that reveals our true identities and find out.

Are you the bumbler whose mayoral campaign launch is dominated by calls to abolish speed bumps and children's booster seats?

The social liberal who strongly supports immigration because multicultural Ancient Athens thrived while xenophobic Sparta – which probably put up provocative posters of Nigel Farage in front of the slogan 'The Achaean League has failed us all' – collapsed?

The unreconstructed right-winger whose *Telegraph* columns so alarm London liberals that the *Guardian*'s headline on your victory is 'New Dusk'?

The depressive loner? Or the gregarious party-goer? The uxorious family man? Or the serial philanderer? The ambitious man-child halfway towards his lifetime ambition to be World King? Or the irreverent journalist apparently terrified by the prospect of becoming Mayor?[92]

The Magic Mirror is so confused that it shatters into a million tiny shards.

The answer, it seems, is that you are all things to most people.

Or at least you're not a five-headed newt gremlin called Ken Livingstone.

Congratulations. You're Mayor of London.

Turn to episode 47

75

'Prime Minister won't be enough for Boris,' says your former tutor at Balliol, Oxford, as you enter Number 10. 'He wants to be [Childlike] emperor.'[93]

As Aristotle said, 'Give me a child until he is twenty-one and I will show you the man-child at fifty-five.'

To help you in this next stage of your imperial quest, you initially have the full support of your reconciled hobgoblin, Michael Gove, and your Luckdragon, Dominic Cummings. Inspired variously by Sun Tzu, Game Theory, 'hard rain' theory and the ingenious 'swerve' methodology (fly fast and don't blink), Cummings's real hero is Bismarck, who attempted to unite Germany by waging simultaneous war on the BBC, the Judiciary, Parliament, the uncodified constitution, the Conservative Party, The Nothing, the DUP and Jeremy Corbyn.

After years of stalemate, you sense an impatience in the country for another vacuous three-word slogan.

'Call an election, you big girl's blouse,'[94] you tell

Corbyn, showing the same sort of twenty-first-century sensitivity displayed by Sir Dave when he told Angela Eagle to 'Calm down, dear'.[95]

It's time to Get Brexit Done.

Despite locking yourself in a fridge, stealing a journalist's phone and refusing to be interviewed by Andrew Neil, ~~the Conservative Party wins more seats than a toxic, divided Labour Party~~ you win an enormous personal mandate to do whatever you want to do for the next five years.

Whatever that might be.

Turn to episode 70

76

Whoops.

Any fule know that being a girly swot is no way to be Topp in Britain.

Down with Skool.

It's the end of the quest for you, you big girl's blouse.

The End

77

Biden's right: you *are* a physical and emotional clone of Trump. But you're increasingly 'convinced that there is method in his madness'.[96]

You win the Democratic nomination for the hotly contested 2020 presidential race, telling the party that the only way to beat the Republican President is to out-Trump him.

You promise to build a wall on the Canadian border.

To impose a travel ban on all countries ending with the letter A.

To withdraw American troops from around the world – and invade China.

To pack the Supreme Court with as many infertile, middle-aged white men as it takes to protect Roe v. Wade.

To trade Puerto Rico for Britain.

To interfere in Russian 'elections'.

To withdraw from the Paris Agreement on Climate Change – and NATO, the IMF, the WHO and the UN.

To 'achieve more notches on your phallocratic phallus'.[97]

To Make America Straight Again.

You catch Covid on the campaign trail. Realizing that you don't have health insurance, you drink bleach on live television. You almost die. And yet still you rise, like a phoenix from the ashes, to win the popular vote, the Electoral College and the Presidency.

This is not how Trump sees it.

Encouraged to 'stop the steal' by marching peacefully on the Capitol while carrying a noose to hang Mike Pence, the Proud Boys head towards Congress. But they haven't reckoned on the Boris Boys marching too.

There is a stand-off on Pennsylvania Avenue.

If you tell the Boris Boys to 'stand back and stand by', turn to episode 27

If you encourage them to 'fight like hell', turn to episode 43

78

Your decision to postpone Covid Freedom Day again provokes the Covid Recovery Group, a loose grouping of Tory Orcs modelled on the European Research Group, into new paroxysms of rage.

'Get Covid Done!' they chant in their strange guttural language, sneezing on each other as they heap discarded facemasks on to a giant bonfire on Parliament Square.

'Keep foreign variants out of Kent!' shouts the *Telegraph*.

'Enemy of the People!' screams the *Daily Mail*, putting a picture of you waving a white flag on their front page.

The All-Seeing, All-Knowing Right-Wing Media is not happy with you.

How, an editorial asks, can you, a seventeen-stone bruiser, be scared of something so small that it's invisible to the naked eye?

You try to stand firm.

But when England loses to Italy in the European Championship final in July 2021, the herd of goblins starts to move.

The tearooms are awash with gossip about your replacement.

Rishi tweets his unswerving support – and promptly hires a dozen more social media specialists to run @ReadyForDishi.

Liz Truss declares her undying devotion – and holds 'Fizz for Liz' dinner parties every night for Tory backbenchers.

Letters of no confidence pour into the 1922 Committee.

You're gone by November, replaced by Mark Harper, who introduces a fourth lockdown the moment the Omicron variant arrives.

In 2022 he's replaced by Liz Truss.

Turn to episode 87

79

All the polls point towards a victory for Remain in the 2016 referendum.

However, the overwhelming majority of Tory voters back Leave.

If you don't support Leave and they win, you'll have missed the quest of a lifetime.

You remove the Childlike Empress's silver amulet from your neck and toss it in the air. It lands snake tails up. You decide to support Leave.

Protestors gather outside your house in Islington.

'He'll need balls of steel,' Rachel texts your wife – and not, for once, because she's going to kick you in them.[98]

On the other side of the argument are twenty-five out of thirty Cabinet members, the majority of Conservative goblins, 73 per cent of all MPs, all previous Prime Ministers, your father, your sister, your brother, more than 1,280 business leaders, the Archwizard of Canterbury and David Beckham.

On your side are Mark Francois, Sol Campbell and your mum.

But you also have your loyal hobgoblin Michael

Gove and his Luckdragon, Dominic Cummings, a talented but deeply divisive creature able to perform extraordinary feats of wizardry, each feat damaging his eyesight a little more.

The Leave campaign relies on sophisticated, modern political techniques: micro-targeted adverts on social media, three-word slogans, dog-whistle racism and lying.

You win with 51.9 per cent of the vote.

'He's ruined my life,' says Sir Dave, who immediately announces his intention to spend more time in his £25,000 shepherd's hut.[99]

The other 48.1 per cent of the country agrees with him.

You are the bookies' favourite to become Prime Minister.

Jamie Oliver threatens to leave the country.* So does Sir Max Hastings.†

But then Michael Gove's wife calls him in for a chat. Rupert Murdoch and Paul Dacre, the Dark Overlords of the All-Seeing, All-Knowing Right-Wing Media, have some concerns about the Boris/Gove ticket.

She writes her husband an email which is accidentally sent to a member of the public. 'You MUST have SPECIFIC assurances from Boris

* He's still here.
† He's still here, too.

OTHERWISE you cannot guarantee your support,' it says. 'Be your stubborn best. GOOD LUCK.'[100]

Maybe YOU'LL tell us in your memoirs just HOW STUBBORN Michael Gove's BEST is.

Despite having known you for thirty years, he suddenly concludes that you cannot 'provide the leadership or build the team for the task ahead'.[101]

Perhaps he has noticed how every successful wish in Fantastica is taking away a part of you – until you're almost no longer human.

Or maybe he just wants to be PM himself.

If you decide to run against him, turn to episode 60

If you reluctantly withdraw, turn to episode 82

80

'Sod Somerset,' you say to Carrie. 'We're off to Kabul.'

She's uneasy about this. Can't you just do what the friend of her friend asks and intervene personally with the Foreign Office, denying claims that you intervened as 'complete nonsense' until a damning paper trail showing that you intervened finally emerges?[102]

No, you say, throwing your Princess a hard look – and a burka. That would be unethical.

August 2021 is not a good time to arrive incognito in Kabul looking for 150 animals, one former Royal Marine and a PR stunt. Hundreds of thousands of people are clamouring to be airlifted out of the Desert of Shattered Hopes. The Taliban is rapidly approaching. Chaos reigns at the airport in scenes already being compared to the US withdrawal from Saigon.

But just think of the positive publicity if you, St Boris of Assisi, bring home the animals personally.

And the useful distraction from the 'serious systemic failures' which characterize the UK government's response.[103]

Besides, you could do with some action – like Winston Churchill in the Anglo-Sudan War or John Simpson 'liberating' Kabul in 2001.

You take Carrie by the hand and push past the tide of annoying people crushed against the airport's perimeter fence in order to reach the poor donkeys in the city beyond.

Strong hands grip you both.

You're hauled over the fence.

Butted by Kalashnikovs.

Bundled into a truck.

Paraded on Taliban TV.

Separated from Carrie, who returns home to Fantastica to marry Michael Gove.

Given four replacement wives.

And, in the latest of a series of remarkable career U-turns, appointed Afghan Minister for the Promotion of Virtue and the Prevention of Vice.

The End

81

By 2016 the only thing you lack is a celebrity wife to go with the celebrity lifestyle.

So you decide to upgrade by marrying into the Royal Family, a useful apprenticeship for a World King.

Having discarded Princess Beatrice for being too old, you settle on wooing Princess Eugenie. In 2018 the crowds cheer as the happy couple flies into Westminster Abbey on the back of a unicorn, with only your best hobgoblin, Michael Gove, whispering in your ear: *'Memento mori.'*

It is wise advice. The following year, you dramatically fall out with your in-laws after Prince William accuses you of making Kate cry after you said that he said that she said that you said he was copying your hairstyle.

You emigrate to America, where you quickly build a successful portfolio media career on Netflix, Spotify and Oprah.

You're now a huge star on both sides of the Atlantic.

Having kept your American citizenship, you decide to make a bid for the White House.

Turn to episode 58

82

Leaning into the Shakespearean motifs embraced by the media while the households of Cameron, Johnson and Gove tear each other apart, you quote the bard's Brutus to explain your decision not to stand for Prime Minister in 2016: '[Now is] a time not to fight the tide of history but to take that tide at the flood and sail on to fortune,' you say.[104]

This is not the only thing you have in common with Brutus.

Hoping it will be a poisoned chalice, Theresa May appoints you Foreign Secretary, a decision greeted by boos at the French embassy, laughter by a German newsreader and rejoicing in Iran.

You swig deeply from that chalice, throwing your diplomatic weight behind the Brexit negotiations by likening President Hollande to a Second World War guard administering 'punishment beatings to anyone who chooses to escape'.[105]

Your deputy refers to himself as 'Silvio Borisconi's pooper-scooper'.[106]

'It is inevitable there is going to be a certain

amount of plaster coming off the ceiling in the chancelleries of Europe,' you say.[107]

You're less World King; more global laughing stock.

You do, however, enjoy one success, taking the lead in expelling 153 Russian diplomats from nearly thirty countries after the Salisbury poisonings in March 2018.

A few weeks later you are invited on your annual jaunt to an enchanted Italian castle owned by the son of an KGB agent.

Nothing to worry about there.

No need to take any officials.

Or security.

Just a 'spouse, family member or friend' – according to the entry of ministerial interests on the Foreign Office website.[108]

A description that covers all manner of sins.

Time to hop on the private jet.

Turn to episode 49

83

In April 2019 you defect from the Lib Dems and join the Independent Group for Change, also known as the Tiggers, also known as Change UK (until Change.org threatened to sue), also known as the worst idea in British politics since the pasty tax.

You decide to give up on politics and return to showbiz. But is your star on the wane?

Turn to episode 23

84

You reluctantly return from Kyiv in June 2022 in time for two by-election defeats and the realization that a prophet is rarely welcome in his own country.

Perhaps you lost the seats because one was held by a convicted paedophile and another by someone looking for tractor porn in the chamber of the House of Goblins (there but for the Grace of God go we all).

Or maybe you've finally run out of wishes.

A third sexual scandal erupts (unusually, none of them involves you directly), concerning a deputy chief whip incapacitated by alcohol and nominative determinism.

Your apology is not enough to stop the herd from moving.

Your rivals claim that they also inherited amulets from the Childlike Empress allowing them to do whatever they wished.

Rishi's ready with his Prada loafers – and his stories about working in the family shop.

Liz is limbering up with her tax cuts – and her white blouse and bow tie tribute act.

Twenty-seven members of the government resign in twenty-four hours.

Another record.

Your third Chancellor lasts a day before joining a Cabinet delegation urging you to stand down.

You go through three Education Secretaries in three days (maybe not the first time you've had three secretaries in three days).

Gove calls to advise you to stand down. You advise him to fuck off back to his Luckdragon, Cummings.

After forty-eight hours, fifty-seven ministers have resigned, shits quitting the sinking rat.

Surely you can't last any longer?

Or can you?

If you decide to stick it out, turn to episode 10

If it's time to resign as PM, turn to episode 54

85

'If I added up the IQ of my father and my mother, don't you think they'd be more than the IQ of your father and mother?' is your excellent chat-up line.

Allegra is smitten. You are engaged before you leave Oxford and married shortly afterwards.

(Your future in-laws are less impressed when you turn up to a family skiing holiday with only a tweed jacket and moleskin trousers, and to your wedding with no morning suit. Your first marriage doesn't last very long.)

Meanwhile, there is a rival for your attention at Oxford. Away from Allegra and the Bullingdon Boys, you spend a lot of your time with the Govester, your loyal hobgoblin stooge and self-declared 'votary of the Boris cult'.[109]

You share an obsession with the enchanted world of British politics, a Fantastica which has little in common with the normal human world inhabited by ordinary mortals. In 1986, this Fantastica is ruled by the Childlike Empress Margaret Thatcher, to whom all neverending Tories owe their existence.

You would both do anything to enter this Fantastica and meet her one day.

In the meantime, Gove helps you take possession of a legendary weapon associated with the rightful sovereignty of Britain. Grasp this glittering prize as a teenager, they say, and the throne is yours.

Many have tried; few succeed.

Congratulations: you have raised Excalibur from the stone; you are President of the Oxford Union.

Turn to episode 11

86

After a light bop on the nose from Sir Gideon, you concede defeat and throw your weight behind Project Fear in the EU referendum.

Vote Remain, you argue, or inflation will soar, climate change will run rife, energy bills will become unpayable, labour shortages will damage the food supply chain, a pandemic will ravage the world, Dover will see six-hour queues, England will lose to Italy in Euro 2020 on penalties, GDP growth will lag behind other G7 countries, Boris Becker will go to jail, red tape will strangle businesses, Russia will invade Ukraine, *Neighbours* will end on TV, the Queen will die and a many-faced Medusa called Liz Truss will become Prime Minister.

The electorate accuses you of scaremongering and votes to Leave.

Six years later, they see how prescient you were. Liz Truss makes you Foreign Secretary. By the summer of 2023 you're being spoken of as a serious challenger for Downing Street.

Turn to episode 44

87

Despite being thrown out of Downing Street, you decide to stay in the House of Goblins for now, taking an MP's salary of £84,144 – aka one month's heating bill.

Liz Truss tries to get you out of her Medusa hair (and her £4.50 earrings from Claire's Accessories) by giving you a peerage, but you're not falling for that one. Why shuffle off to the Land of Ghosts when you can 'support her every step of the way'[110] by making life awkward for her on the green benches?

You're going to emulate your predecessors, Theresa May, Gordon Brown and Ted Heath – although God help you if you're going to waste the rest of your life skulking and sulking around this godforsaken place.

You're the Father of the Nation, not the Father of the House.

You're King Arthur, licking his wounds on Avalon. You're Bilbo Baggins, banished from the mountain by Thorin. You're Winston Churchill in 1945.

And now you're going to win the peace, as well as the war.

By February 2023, everyone agrees with Cummings that, despite considerable competition, Liz Truss is as 'close to properly crackers'[111] as any other goblin in Parliament.

To tackle an inflation rate of 28 per cent, Suella Braverman, Truss's fourth Chancellor, cuts the top rate of tax to 5p – and abolishes universal credit.

When the Governor of the Bank of England raises interest rates by an unprecedented five percentage points, Truss lambasts him for 'Failing. To. Believe. In. Britain.'

Having led the country to these 'unlit uplands',[112] her net approval ratings are minus 60. Yours have been gently climbing.

Time to go on manoeuvres.

You ask backbench MPs for 'Beer with Boris'.

You sit on Rishi until he promises to register @BorisIsBack.

When Russia gears up to invade Estonia in April, you travel to Fulton, Missouri, where you give a well-received speech in Estonian, Latvian, Lithuanian and English about the new Iron Curtain descending on the continent.

Your *Sikanda* is on fire.

In July you replace Truss as PM, winning thumping support from nostalgic Tories both inside and outside Parliament.

'This. Is. A. Disgrace,' says Truss, tearfully, outside

Downing Street – before defecting to (re)join the Lib Dems.

You call an election in 2024, having elevated Nadine Dorries, the Member for Mid-Loonyshire, to the City of Ghosts and taken over her much safer seat for yourself.

Turn to episode 28

88

You hear nothing from the Russians for a while. Maybe they think your political career is over after you resign from the Cabinet in July 2018 over May's Brexit deal.

But then, one year later, you unexpectedly become Prime Minister of the Fantastica of Great Britain.

Suddenly the Russian ogres are back in touch.

Undermine trust in British democracy by proroguing Parliament, they say, *or we'll release the kompromat.*

Endanger peace in Northern Ireland by erecting a border in the Irish Sea, or the world gets to see the tapes.

Call an election and get rid of our embarrassing spokesperson Mr Corbyn.

Ignore Covid, wash your hands and sing 'Happy Birthday' instead.

Undermine social cohesion by throwing a party in the middle of lockdown.

Make Londongrad – and especially the Conservative Party coffers – a comfortable destination for questionable Russian money.

The ogres' spell is so powerful that you go along

with all these outrageous demands. But when the Russians ~~invade Ukraine~~ carry out a 'special military operation' inside Ukraine's borders, in order to take the pressure of Partygate off their best-placed foreign agent, the demands become increasingly difficult to fulfil.

The Kremlin wants you to resist European sanctions, send aid to the Russian military and bail out Chelsea Football Club.

You refuse. You're not an appeaser.

The Childlike Empress wouldn't let herself be pushed around by the Russians like this.

Summing up all your strength from her amulet, you try to resist the ogres' spell.

You are the Iron Baby.

But when an invitation comes through to visit the Peter and Paul Cathedral in St Petersburg, 'famous not just in Europe, but in the whole world, for its 123-metre spire', the alarm bells really start ringing.

You decide to call the Russians' bluff. How bad could the tapes be?

You double your security detail.

You train Dilyn the Jack Russell to nip everyone who enters the building – and not just Rishi.

You get Priti Patel to send anyone whose surname ends in -*ov* to Rwanda.

All to no avail.

You *want* to go to that diplomatic function.

You *really* want that third, glistening vol-au-vent, even if the first two tasted a bit funny.

And that fourth Ferrero Rocher.

'Mr Ambassador,' you say, 'you are spoiling us.'

These are your final words.

The End

89

It is possible, you realize, to 'have a pretty good life being a leech and a parasite in the media world, gadding about from TV studio to TV studio, writing inconsequential pieces and having a good time'.[113]

Whereas your British self might find this unsatisfying, here in supersize-me America you embrace it wholeheartedly. You have sucked from the sugary teat of fame and you want more. You talk about 'your truth' on Oprah. You write seventy-one prequels to *Seventy-two Virgins*, winning *Literary Review*'s Bad Sex in Fiction Award four times more than your sister (although critics still prefer Rachel's victorious entry: 'a strange animal noise escapes from me as the mounting, Wagnerian crescendo overtakes me').[114]

You're not going to be World King any more. But you're content with simply ruling the airwaves.

But then, one day, your ratings begin to slide. You lose your job to Piers Morgan, who loses his job to the thin bloke who used to be the fat bloke in *Gavin & Stacey*.

A bloated leech, you can suckle no more.

You are cast out of Manhattan.

Like Lancelot, you 'wander footloose in outlandish parts'.

Idaho. Kansas. Oklahoma.

You are last seen begging Harry, the Prince formerly known as HRH, and Meghan, the maiden formerly known as paralegal Rachel Zane in *Suits*, for a walk-on part in *Tiger King 7*.

They say no.

The End

90

'Delaware, Dela-*where*?' you quip, alienating another 740,977 people.

But defeat has at least galvanized your American quest. It is to seek power. Power at all costs. Power for the sake of power.

Potentia gratia potentiae.

(Yes, that's the correct use of the genitive.)

Later you might work out what to do with all this power.

However, American politics is clearly a tough nut to crack. You're going to need a bigger profile before running again.

Fortunately, your reporting from Washington DC has caught the eye of a fraudulent newspaper magnate we shall call Robert Maxwell because he is dead and therefore harder to libel than other newspaper magnates who have given you jobs over the years.

He gives you the editorship of one of his flagship national magazines, the *American Sextator*.

In an editorial in 2004, your magazine lambasts the 'mawkish sentimentality' of Detroit, Michigan, a city on the wrong coast 'wallowing in a sense of vicarious victimhood' during its long-term slide into economic decline.[115]

Detroit isn't happy.

If you decide to go to Detroit to apologize in person, turn to episode 35

If you keep your head low, turn to episode 26

91

In September 2023 you take over from Jens Stoltenberg as Secretary General of NATO.

In October 2023 you invade Russia.

The End (of the World)

92

You serve a full, successful and uneventful second term as London Mayor, retiring from the political world of Fantastica in 2016 having built 94,001 affordable homes, reduced poverty, raised the living wage and introduced a successful apprenticeship scheme.

You remain resolutely neutral in the 2016 referendum campaign, helping a fractured and fractious country to rally round the Prime Minister after a narrow victory for Remain.

You give the Childlike Empress's amulet to Sir Dave.

You don't need it any more. You know your own wishes now – your only wish. It is no longer to be wise or strong or powerful or loved. It is simply to love.

Sometimes you return briefly to Fantastica to sit in the Land of Ghosts, speaking wisely and calmly on topics close to your heart, such as the reform of state education.

Whenever you claim your £323 per day attendance allowance, you donate it to a food bank charity.

But you spend most of your time in Oxford, becoming Master of Balliol College and writing a series of erudite and learned books on the Ancient World.

You are often compared to Cincinnatus, the Roman leader who relinquished power to return to his plough – although, unlike him, you stay there.

Interviewed by a troll on the *Southern Oracle*, you gently scold him when he tries to label you 'the Great Knower' or the 'Knight of the Seven-armed Candelabrum' or 'Saviour' or simply 'Boris'.

'Call me by my name,' you say. 'Call me Alexander.'

You don't catch Covid.

Neither do quite so many other people.

You're not World King.

You're not even the Childlike Emperor.

But you are happy.

And so are the rest of us.

The End

Notes

1   Gimson, Andrew, *Boris: The Making of the Prime Minister*, Simon & Schuster, London, 2016, p. 8.

2   https://hansard.parliament.uk/Commons/2021-12-08/debates/45C3B261-14F7-4DDC-A7D8-EB8A76097CFB/Engagements

3   Interview with Michael Cockerell, BBC, 25 March 2013; quoted in Mount, Harry (ed.), *The Wit and Wisdom of Boris Johnson*, Bloomsbury, London, 2019, p. 3.

4   Bower, Tom, *Boris Johnson: The Gambler*, W.H. Allen, London, 2020, p. 239.

5   Ibid., p. 265.

6   Purcell, Sonia, *Just Boris: The Irresistible Rise of a Political Celebrity*, Aurum, London, 2011, p. 102.

7   Gimson, Andrew, *Boris: The Making of the Prime Minister*, Simon & Schuster, London, 2016, p. 43.

8   Bower, Tom, *Boris Johnson: The Gambler*, W.H. Allen, London, 2020, p. 88. You double down on your denial of this affair, responding to allegations by saying, 'I am amazed people can write this drivel.' This denial is, in itself, somewhat amazing.

9   Ibid., p. 69.

10   https://www.thearticle.com/what-really-went-on-at-boris-johnsons-spectator-lunches

11   Mount, Harry (ed.), *The Wit and Wisdom of Boris Johnson*, Bloomsbury, London, 2019, p. 24.

12   Bower, Tom, *Boris Johnson: The Gambler*, W.H. Allen, London, 2020, p. 105.

13   Ibid., p. 106. Although you declare that you're laying down your pen, you don't mention your magical *Sikanda*. Maybe you want to keep it secret.

14   Mount, Harry (ed.), *The Wit and Wisdom of Boris Johnson*, Bloomsbury, London, 2019, p. 77. You say this to schoolchildren in Norwood in March 2013. It's possible they don't understand what you mean either.

15   Interview in the *Radio Times*, 19 March 2013, https://www.radiotimes.com/tv/current-affairs/boris-johnson-id-love-to-have-a-crack-at-being-prime-minister/. To translate for non-rugby enthusiasts, this metaphor means you would sell your own grandmother in order to further your own career.

16   Mount, Harry (ed.), *The Wit and Wisdom of Boris Johnson*, Bloomsbury, London, 2019, p. 10. The *Eton Chronicle* includes a similar version of this chant in a report on the Wall Game.

17   Ibid., p. 90. As London Mayor you meet Hillary Clinton in 2015, eight years after these comments. She professes herself 'pleased by some aspects of the article' (https://www.theguardian.com/politics/2015/feb/11/boris-johnson-sings-hillary-clinton-praises).

18   https://www.theguardian.com/commentisfree/2022/sep/04/boris-johnson-dreams-comeback-nightmare-liz-truss

19   https://www.theguardian.com/politics/2017/feb/08/boris-johnson-renounces-us-citizenship-record-2016-uk-foreign-secretary

20   https://www.telegraph.co.uk/politics/2018/06/23/eu-diplomats-shocked-boris-four-letter-reply-business-concerns/

21   *Desert Island Discs*, October 2005; quoted in Mount,
     Harry (ed.), *The Wit and Wisdom of Boris Johnson*,
     Bloomsbury, London, 2019, p. 29.

22   Mount, Harry (ed.), *The Wit and Wisdom of Boris Johnson*,
     Bloomsbury, London, 2019, p. 145. Extraordinarily, this
     is a genuine extract from a rap performed by Michael
     Gove in March 2018 at your future third wife's thirtieth
     birthday party (you are a sprightly fifty-three). Sadly, no
     video evidence exists, although you might still enjoy
     googling 'Michael Gove rap', for old times' sake.

23   https://dominiccummings.com/2020/01/02/two-hands-
     are-a-lot-were-hiring-data-scientists-project-managers-
     policy-experts-assorted-weirdos/

24   https://metro.co.uk/2022/01/31/dominic-cummings-says-
     ousting-boris-is-an-unpleasant-duty-16020636/. In
     another life, this is how Dominic Cummings shows his
     appreciation for being hired – and fired – by you.

25   Mount, Harry (ed.), *The Wit and Wisdom of Boris Johnson*,
     Bloomsbury, London, 2019, p. 105. This is not the only
     time you deploy what you call your 'Tottometer'
     (although surely Tottymeter is a better name). In 1997
     your 'Tottometer' reports that there are more beautiful
     women at the Labour Party conference, while in 2001
     you believe that the Tories 'are fighting back in a big way'.

26   Bower, Tom, *Boris Johnson: The Gambler*, W.H. Allen,
     London, 2020, p. 315.

27   https://www.reuters.com/world/uk/uk-denies-report-that-
     pm-johnson-said-let-bodies-pile-high-2021-04-26/

28   Bower, Tom, *Boris Johnson: The Gambler*, W.H. Allen,
     London, 2020, p. 71.

29   Gill, A. A., *Sunday Times*; quoted by Michael Wolff in
     Vanity Fair, 29 April 2008 (https://www.vanityfair.com/
     news/2004/09/wolff200409).

30   Purcell, Sonia, *Just Boris: The Irresistible Rise of a Political Celebrity*, Aurum, London, 2011, p. 230.

31   Ibid., p. 233.

32   Bower, Tom, *Boris Johnson: The Gambler*, W.H. Allen, London, 2020, p. 76.

33   Interview in the *Daily Mirror*; quoted in Bower, Tom, *Boris Johnson: The Gambler*, W.H. Allen, London, 2020, p. 79.

34   https://www.independent.co.uk/voices/boris-johnson-general-election-islamophobia-conservative-muslim-brexit-a9092896.html

35   Mount, Harry (ed.), *The Wit and Wisdom of Boris Johnson*, Bloomsbury, London, 2019, p. 101. This is how you describe the press in 2008 while running for Mayor of London.

36   Johnson, Boris, *Lend Me Your Ears*, Harper Perennial, London, 2004, p. 3.

37   Bower, Tom, *Boris Johnson: The Gambler*, W.H. Allen, London, 2020, p. 265.

38   Ibid., pp. 75–6.

39   Ibid., p. 220. In 2013, on a trip to Beijing, you and George Osborne do actually have a fight in a lift. It is not recorded who wins.

40   Ibid., p. 86. 'A pilgrimage of penitence' is how you describe your trip to Liverpool following the editorial in *The Spectator*. You're not murdered in Liverpool, although you are called a 'self-centred pompous twit' during a radio interview.

41   Ibid., p. 36.

42   Ibid., p. 42. This 'quote', which saw you sacked from *The Times* in London in 1988, has been moved to an American scenario, making it only slightly more fabricated than the original.

43 https://metro.co.uk/video/slava-ukraini-boris-johnson-signs-commons-statement-willing-glory-ukraine-2622711/

44 https://www.theatlantic.com/magazine/archive/2021/07/boris-johnson-minister-of-chaos/619010/

45 Mount, Harry (ed.), *The Wit and Wisdom of Boris Johnson*, Bloomsbury, London, 2019, p. 149. This is what Ian Hislop, one of the regular team captains on *Have I Got News for You*, says about you. It is possible – but unlikely – that David Letterman says it too.

46 https://www.theguardian.com/uk-news/2022/jun/20/no-10-confirms-asked-the-times-drop-carrie-johnson-story

47 Bower, Tom, *Boris Johnson: The Gambler*, W.H. Allen, London, 2020, p. 273. This is what David Cameron calls Dominic Cummings – although he doesn't, as far as anyone is aware, refer to him as a psychopathic Luckdragon.

48 Mount, Harry (ed.), *The Wit and Wisdom of Boris Johnson*, Bloomsbury, London, 2019, p. 79.

49 Ibid., p. 41. Despite making this same tantalizing promise to Tory voters in 2005, your party loses the general election.

50 Ibid., p. 120. You use this line in an interview in the *Daily Telegraph* in 2004. Having an intermittent Christian faith causes fewer problems in Britain than in rural West Virginia.

51 https://www.theatlantic.com/magazine/archive/2021/07/boris-johnson-minister-of-chaos/619010/. A friend of yours once told a journalist that you subscribe to a pre-Christian morality system with 'no clear set of rules'. You deny this, describing yourself instead as a 'kind of very, very bad Christian'.

52 Mount, Harry (ed.), *The Wit and Wisdom of Boris Johnson*, Bloomsbury, London, 2019, p. 120.

53 Bower, Tom, *Boris Johnson: The Gambler*, W.H. Allen, London, 2020, p. 164.

54 Interview in the *Daily Telegraph*, 6 June 2008; quoted in Mount, Harry (ed.), *The Wit and Wisdom of Boris Johnson*, Bloomsbury, London, 2019, p. 62.

55 https://www.theguardian.com/politics/blog/2008/aug/19/borisaccusescameronoftalki

56 Bower, Tom, *Boris Johnson: The Gambler*, W.H. Allen, London, 2020, p. 160. This is not the last time Rachel brings tits into politics. In 2019 she says 'Boobs to Brexit' by removing her blouse on Sky News (https://www.plymouthherald.co.uk/news/uk-world-news/rachel-johnson-says-boobs-brexit-2548454). It doesn't stop Brexit Getting Done.

57 https://www.independent.co.uk/tv/news/cummings-says-boris-wanted-to-get-whitty-to-inject-him-with-covid-live-on-tv-ve6ab24f5. Yes, you actually suggested this.

58 https://www.opendemocracy.net/en/opendemocracyuk/revealed-boris-russian-oligarch-and-page-3-model/

59 https://www.bbc.co.uk/news/uk-politics-62308217

60 https://www.theguardian.com/politics/2019/jul/26/boris-johnson-security-evgeny-lebedev-perugia-party

61 https://www.politicshome.com/news/article/boris-johnson-bond-villain-nato-tobias-ellwood

62 Bower, Tom, *Boris Johnson: The Gambler*, W.H. Allen, London, 2020, p. 231.

63 https://www.theguardian.com/books/2014/nov/03/churchill-factor-review-boris-johnson-winston

64 https://www.theguardian.com/books/2014/nov/03/churchill-factor-review-boris-johnson-winston

65 https://www.independent.co.uk/arts-entertainment/books/reviews/the-churchill-factor-how-one-man-made-history-by-boris-johnson-book-review-all-about-our-greatest-leader-and-a-bit-about-churchill-9816767.html

66 https://www.theguardian.com/politics/video/2013/mar/24/boris-johnson-accused-nasty-video

67 Bower, Tom, *Boris Johnson: The Gambler*, W.H. Allen, London, 2020, p. 174.

68 https://www.dailymail.co.uk/news/article-10993517/DAILY-MAIL-COMMENT-Boris-faced-end-rueful-smile-Tory-party-live-regret-it.html

69 https://www.lesechos.fr/idees-debats/en-vue/liz-truss-une-girouette-de-fer-1775739

70 https://www.reuters.com/world/uk/booster-rocket-or-roman-dictator-boris-johnson-says-farewell-now-2022-09-06/

71 https://www.telegraph.co.uk/news/election-2010/7186038/General-Election-2010-Gordon-Brown-will-be-in-power-for-ever-if-Nick-Clegg-gets-PR.html

72 https://news.sky.com/story/boris-compares-eu-ambitions-to-those-of-hitler-10282334. In another life, when you're campaigning to Leave the EU, you echo Rees-Mogg's comparisons almost exactly.

73 Bower, Tom, *Boris Johnson: The Gambler*, W.H. Allen, London, 2020, pp. 270–1. You're less kind towards Barack Obama's heritage when he makes the case for Britain remaining in the EU.

74 Ibid., p. 275. To be fair, you actually write this limerick for *The Spectator* in May 2016, two months *before* you're made Foreign Secretary, winning £1,000 from the magazine you used to edit in its 'most offensive Erdoğan poem' competition. Instead of being sacked, you're promoted by Theresa May. Here are your diplomatic gems in full: *There*

*was a young fellow from Ankara / Who was a terrific Wankerer /
Till he sowed his wild oats / With the help of a goat / But he
didn't even stop to thankera.*

75   Mount, Harry (ed.), *The Wit and Wisdom of Boris Johnson*,
Bloomsbury, London, 2019, p. 147. You make a similar
pledge in the run-up to the 2019 general election,
referring to the 'Scylla and Charybdis' of Corbyn and
Farage. During the election campaign itself, you and
Cummings opt for a simpler three-word slogan.

76   https://www.nbcnews.com/think/opinion/biden-
meets-trump-mini-me-boris-johnson-first-time-can-
ncna1270153

77   https://www.standard.co.uk/news/uk/dominic-raab-
foreign-secretary-kabul-taliban-sky-news-b952228.html

78   https://www.dailymail.co.uk/news/article-3671749/
RACHEL-JOHNSON-Mrs-Gove-detonated-bomb-
blew-Boris.html

79   https://www.independent.co.uk/news/uk/politics/theresa-
may-margaret-thatcher-jeremy-corbyn-first-pmqs-
remind-him-of-anybody-a7146141.html

80   Bower, Tom, *Boris Johnson: The Gambler*, W.H. Allen,
London, 2020, p. 352. This is, of course, what you,
Theresa May's Foreign Secretary, call her Brexit deal.

81   Ibid., p. 101. You describe yourself as a 'one-man melting
pot' (the melting pot of Eton, Oxford and the *Daily
Telegraph*?) in an article in the *Evening Standard* setting
out your stall to be Mayor of London.

82   Ibid., pp. 101, 104. This is an amalgamation of various
comments you make about bendy buses in London. You
really don't like them.

83   https://www.express.co.uk/news/politics/524156/Boris-
Johnson-I-have-more-in-common-three-toed-sloth-
Churchill

84 Bower, Tom, *Boris Johnson: The Gambler*, W.H. Allen, London, 2020, p. 194.

85 Ibid., p. 194.

86 Gimson, Andrew, *Boris: The Making of the Prime Minister*, Simon & Schuster, London, 2016, p. 22.

87 Bower, Tom, *Boris Johnson: The Gambler*, W.H. Allen, London, 2020, p. 354.

88 Ibid., p. 354.

89 Ibid., p. 364.

90 Mount, Harry (ed.), *The Wit and Wisdom of Boris Johnson*, Bloomsbury, London, 2019, p. 114. This is not the only time you dream of turning back the clock to 1904. During the launch of the Barclays hire scheme in 2010, you longingly point out that 20 per cent of London journeys were made by bicycle in 1904.

91 https://www.theguardian.com/politics/2022/jan/26/ambushed-with-a-cake-defence-of-boris-johnson-inspires-mirth

92 Bower, Tom, *Boris Johnson: The Gambler*, W.H. Allen, London, 2020, p. 113.

93 Ibid., p. 393. Another Balliol professor is so furious about your dishonest championing of Brexit that he sends you a formal Latin *renuntiatio amicitiae*, which loosely translates as 'fuck the fuck off'.

94 https://www.bbc.co.uk/news/uk-49593110

95 https://www.theguardian.com/politics/2011/apr/27/david-cameron-calm-down-dear

96 Bower, Tom, *Boris Johnson: The Gambler*, W.H. Allen, London, 2020, p. 343.

97 Mount, Harry (ed.), *The Wit and Wisdom of Boris Johnson*, Bloomsbury, London, 2019, p. 8. Achieving more notches on your 'phallocratic phallus' is your stated

ambition in the Eton Leavers' book. It is one ambition that you largely fulfil.

98 Bower, Tom, *Boris Johnson: The Gambler*, W.H. Allen, London, 2020, p. 266.

99 Ibid., p. 267.

100 https://www.theguardian.com/politics/2016/jun/29/michael-goves-wife-doubts-boris-johnson-email-sarah-vine-dacre-murdoch

101 https://www.theguardian.com/politics/2016/jun/30/goves-leadership-bid-statement-in-full

102 https://www.dailymail.co.uk/news/article-10443611/Boris-Johnson-DID-intervene-help-Pen-Farthing-animal-charity-escape-Taliban-emails-show.html

103 https://committees.parliament.uk/committee/78/foreign-affairs-committee/news/171010/systemic-failures-of-leadership-planning-and-preparation-mps-slam-government-role-in-uk-withdrawal-from-afghanistan/

104 Bower, Tom, *Boris Johnson: The Gambler*, W.H. Allen, London, 2020, p. 290.

105 Ibid., p. 317.

106 Ibid., pp. 302, 308.

107 Ibid., p. 303.

108 https://www.theguardian.com/politics/2019/jul/26/boris-johnson-security-evgeny-lebedev-perugia-party

109 https://www.theguardian.com/news/2022/apr/19/oxford-union-created-ruling-political-class-boris-johnson-michael-gove-theresa-may-rees-mogg

110 https://www.gov.uk/government/speeches/boris-johnsons-final-speech-as-prime-minister-6-september-2022

111 https://unherd.com/2022/05/dominic-cummings-i-dont-like-parties/

112 https://www.theguardian.com/commentisfree/2022/sep/02/festival-of-brexit-unboxed-disaster

113 Morgan, Piers, *Misadventures of a Big Mouth Brit*, Ebury, London, 2010, p. 95.

114 https://literaryreview.co.uk/call-me-sukie

115 https://www.spectator.co.uk/article/bigley-s-fate. A 2004 editorial in *The Spectator*, which you edit, ascribes these characteristics to Liverpool.

Acknowledgements

I owe a considerable debt of gratitude to Charlie Campbell, my agent at Greyhound Literary, who not only came up with the idea for this book, but also trusted me to write it. Huge thanks, too, to Kate Fox and everyone at Transworld (not least to Dan Akers who came up with the title, which was far better than anything I would have managed). Kate has been a wonderful editor from start to finish, improving the mediocre jokes, gently getting rid of the bad ones and even finding a lawyer with a sense of humour. I am also grateful to Dan Balado for his tight copy-editing and impressive knowledge of Ancient Greek etymology, and to Lee Binding for his brilliant cover design.

I spent the summer reading an unusual mixture of fantasy adventure stories and biographies of Boris Johnson. In the latter category, I especially enjoyed Tom Bower's surprisingly even-handed account. For the true fusion of these two genres, however, I am looking forward to the autobiography from the World King himself.

About the author

Iain Hollingshead is a novelist, journalist and teacher of history and politics. He devised and edited a best-selling series of unpublished letters to the *Daily Telegraph*, starting with *Am I Alone in Thinking...?* This series has run for over thirteen years and sold in excess of 300,000 copies. *Blair on Broadway*, his co-written musical, transferred to the West End and included appearances from Sir Derek Jacobi, Matthew Parris and Lembit Öpik. Like Norman Mailer, Tom Wolfe and Rachel (but not yet Boris) Johnson, he is the winner of *Literary Review*'s Bad Sex in Fiction Award.

Other books in the series

Boris Johnson's Day(s) Off

Double Decker Truss

Gove Will Tear us Apart

Cameron Eileen

Osborne in the USA

With or Without EU

It's My Party and I'll Lie if I Want To

No, Prime Minister